Superstar Teacher

A Guide to Enhance Creativity in the Classroom

by

EBONY T. HOLLAND

Watersprings
PUBLISHING

Superstar Teacher
Published by Watersprings Publishing, a division of
Watersprings Media House, LLC.
P.O. Box 1284
Olive Branch, MS 38654
www.waterspringsmedia.com
Contact publisher for bulk orders and permission requests.

Printed in the United States of America.

Library of Congress Control Number: 2021904243

ISBN-13: 978-1-948877-72-5

Cover Photo: Natasha Henry, Photographer of N.H. Photography

Table of Contents

CHAPTER 1

The Making of a Superstar

D o you ever think of children and it brings tears of happiness to your eyes? Do you get excited when a student masters a concept? Do you dream about your students? Do you stay up all night trying to figure out how you can help a student? Do you spend your summers writing lesson plans or thinking of ways to make your classroom better? Do you think about what you will wear to school the next day while sleeping? Do you wait for Walmart or Target to put out the school supplies and buy everything? Y'all, I'm getting excited just typing this!!! Just a few more questions... Do you shop online for tons and tons of resource books and realize that you already have them? Do you plan what your classroom will look like before the school year ends? Do you absolutely love AC Moore, Michaels, Office Depot, Staples, or CVS? Do Crayola crayons and Ticonderoga pencils get you excited? Or how about going to the Education Store or Lakeshore Learning? Well, if you answered yes to any of these questions, then we can be great teacher friends!!!

When did you know that you wanted to be a teacher? Did you decide when you were in grade school or did you wait until it was time to choose a major in college? I come from a family of five girls and one boy. The boy is the oldest. My mother was a single mother, but she raised us with all of the love she could give. She knew how to make each of us feel special. In my family, I never knew of anyone who had ever gone to college after high school. They either went to serve in the Army or Air Force, or just took a job at a mechanic shop, or took up a trade. My grandmother had 8 children and most of them either barely finished high school, or didn't finish at all. It's not that they didn't want to, times were hard back then. My mother had to stop school at an early age in seventh grade to help support her family. Although she could not finish grade school, she was still very smart. She taught us all she knew. She did her best to help us with homework as we got older. Sometimes it was hard not having anyone at home to help, but through it all and with my mother's prayers, we all graduated from high school. I knew that I wanted to go to college and become a teacher, so I could somehow be the motivation to help the rest of my family finish school. I wanted to set the example that we can be educated no matter the circumstances.

I remember we all had to move into my grandmother's house because our house caught fire. She lived in a three-room, shotgun house in New Orleans. It was my mom and four of her kids, my grandmother and her last three sons, that equals nine people in a one-bedroom house. Oh, and I can't forget our dog Ekeey. It was crowded in there, but we survived. Love got us through.

When I was in third grade, I had a teacher named Miss Provost. She was the sweetest person, but firm. She was kind and always helped me in whatever way she could, even down to helping to pay my tuition and buying me a school sweater. She was fun, creative, and smart. I also thought she was pretty. For some strange reason, I admired her because she wore braces. I think because I always wanted braces, a broken arm, and a Jeri curl, but that's another book...hehehehe!!! The way she taught her class always made me feel smart, although sometimes it was difficult for me to understand. I understood her body language and I felt as if I could read her mind, that's how much I studied her. Her teaching methods always mesmerized me. I never wanted to miss a day of school because I wanted to see what new and exciting thing she would introduce that day, and what clothes she would wear. Although there were other students in the class, she made me feel like I was the only one there. When she had to step out of the class, sometimes she would leave me in charge. And man, oh man, I would instantly become her. It was something about standing in front of the class, writing on the board (btw, she loved my handwriting), and assisting other students that made me feel soooo happy and comfortable. I knew right away that I had to have my very own classroom one day. I wanted to be a teacher, just like Miss Provost.

I found pleasure in playing school with my sisters and friends. When we would play outside, I always found myself with our neighborhood friends sitting on the front porch giving instructions on how we would play games or what we would do next. They sat intently and listened to what I had to say. I always had a notebook and a pen writing down what we could do for the summer days. Even though the games we played outside were hide and seek, jacks, house, jump rope, or hopscotch, I ALWAYS found a way to make "school" be one of the games...LOL! Somehow, they let me be the teacher. If they didn't want to cooperate, I'd go get my stuffed animals and dolls and teach them. Someway, somehow, I'd get to teach. I'd go to bed dreaming of what we would do for the next day. I knew my sisters were tired of me, but they tolerated all of my antics.

After completing high school, I was on my way to college. I already knew what I would major in for me there was no other job than to become a teacher. I realized that I loved children so much, but there was a problem. How would we pay for me to go to school? I knew what school I wanted to go to, but where would the money come from? My mom was on welfare and she worked cleaning people's houses, so there was no way I wanted to stress her out. We prayed about it and packed me up, and I headed to my first choice, Oakwood College in Huntsville, AL. We got a ride with a church member (we didn't have a car) who was taking her daughter. We applied for student loans, I got some extra help because my grades were good, and we found other scholarships by just asking questions. Ask and you shall receive. I finally cleared and got a room in Cunningham Hall, then I

Ask and you shall receive.

was moved to Carter Hall. I was enrolled in college. I was the first in my entire family to go to college. OH MY!! I did it, and I was so proud! You don't know how much this meant to me. It was a dream come true. I could finally be the teacher I had always dreamed of becoming, but plans don't always turn out the way you want them to.

A Quick Detour

A hobby of mine is singing. I love to sing. My mother used to sing in a group, my uncle sings and has albums, and my sister Dionne had a single hit out on the radio in New Orleans. Growing up, I sang in the church choir, at school, and in different groups around the city. I guess you can say I come from a family of singers.

While in college, my sophomore year to be exact, I was offered a singing contract on a major record label out of New York. My younger sister Karima had graduated from high school and decided to attend the same college as me. Talk about singers, THIS GIRL CAN SAAANG!! Long story short, a big record executive heard us singing at a program at school. She said, "hadn't heard singing like ours in a long time". My sister along with two other girls and I signed the contract and we became Virtue. We immediately began to record our debut album and started touring the world singing. It was that simple. I was still in school and taking classes, I wouldn't let anything keep me from getting my degree. But I was worried that my dream of becoming a teacher may not happen.

I had understanding professors who allowed me to take my work with me on the road. Thank you so much to another teacher who has left a lasting impression on me, Professor Barbara Warren, who I modeled my teaching after. Her teaching style solidified what I wanted to do all along. I loved going to her class. I loved my student teaching. I loved being able to use what I learned in her class in an actual classroom. I found that the students loved me and that I truly loved them. She told me I was a natural-born teacher and that you don't find many students who are as comfortable as I am in the classroom. Practicing on my sisters and neighborhood friends paid off. My mentoring teacher also said the same thing. I worked under a teacher named Mrs. Delma Harvey in a multi-grade 1st-3rd grade class. I had heard of two grades in one class, but three?! And the icing on the cake, these students were talented and gifted. I was up for the challenge and excelled. Day in and day out, I was challenged to be creative and innovative with these gifted students. I had to think out of the box because they were little "brainiacs." They craved hard work and ate it up all while looking for dessert.

I worked really hard at my student teaching. I overworked myself because I knew that right after class on Fridays, I would be on the next flight out to sing. I would not have time to grade papers on the weekend or do anything school-related. We traveled mainly on the weekends singing, but there were several times during the week we'd be gone as well. We were under contract now, so we were obligated to promote our new CD. I was always in awe that I could be in three states in one day...going from church to church or radio station to radio station. Tired on Monday morning, I'd be right back in the classroom. But as soon as I saw my students, that magic energy would appear and I'd take the stage, but this time it was my classroom stage. There in that classroom, I would light up as if I were on stage. I knew that when I entered that class, I'd better be "lights on" ACTION! The Superstar that I was on stage, could be the same Superstar in the class.

This continued for a few years. I was getting extremely excited because my senior year was on the horizon. My dream of becoming a teacher was in the near

> The Superstar that I was on stage, could be the same Superstar in the class.

future. The requirements for graduating were met. I did not owe any money, Thank God! Although it took me 5 years to finish, I DID IT! I graduated from college. I was the first person in my family to do so. I was one proud graduate.

After graduating college, I was still on the road with Virtue. I found out that I could continue to pursue my education online so I took all of the necessary steps to get my Master's in Education Administration and Supervision from the University of Phoenix. With this degree, I would eventually open up a state-of-the-art daycare center after teaching for a few years. When there was downtime for Virtue, I made sure I was signed up as a substitute teacher in the local schools. I had to somehow keep my dream of becoming a teacher alive, although I was not in my very own classroom. I always felt deep inside that being in a classroom was where I should be, so I never gave up on my dream of having my very own classroom.

I toured and traveled for almost 12 years. Whenever I was in front of children singing, I'd always cry. I just couldn't help myself. They looked so innocent and sweet. Their eyes bright and cheerful, hanging on to every word that I sang... blank slates, ready to soak up knowledge. On stage, I still could see myself in my very own classroom.

I was given several opportunities to help students. While on the road with Virtue, we mentored students in schools. I did everything to work toward my teaching dream. I needed to be around students, so I wouldn't forget all that I had learned. I helped create an after-school program to help students with their homework. I even assisted in starting a school. I was an administrator and Kindergarten-2nd grade teacher. It was a great program. The Superstar was back in the classroom. But duty called for me to be on the road, and my time in the classroom once again ended.

Another Detour

After getting married to the love of my life Skip, in 2002 and having a bouncing baby boy in 2004 named Stinger, the traveling kind of picked up and then slowed down a bit. By this time, I had been living in Maryland for three years. I was not thinking of teaching. I just wanted to spend all of my time with this cute kid of ours.

When my son turned 3, I thought it was time for him to begin school, so I started my search for the best one. The school that I found for him was a private Christian school. Guess what? They just so happened to have a position open for a first-grade teacher. This news excited me!!! I did my research and found a way to get an interview for the open position. I had been out of school for more than 8 years and I was rusty. I was so excited about the interview that I showed up two days early. Can you believe that? My interview was on Thursday, not Tuesday... silly me. I knew it was one of the T's... LOL!! So they told me to come back on Thursday. You better believe, I wore the same outfit that I had on Tuesday because I didn't want to jinx it... LOL... I'm from New Orleans, I can't help it.

When I returned, my interviewers were ready for me. To my surprise, they knew who I was...I guess because of Virtue. They said they loved my music, but also did research on my educational background and loved what they found. We shot the breeze for a few minutes and got acquainted. I was afraid they'd ask me questions that I didn't know the answer to. I sat there with two intelligent women who had pleasant faces, one was the principal of the school and the other from the school board. I answered all of the questions to my ability. What is your teaching style? How do you deal with discipline problems? What are the 4 types of learning styles? Do you even like children? How will you handle singing and teaching? What is cooperative learning? OMG!! My heart stopped! I drew a blank...I could not remember what the answer to that question was. I was honest with my interviewers and told them, I could not remember the answer to cooperative learning. If you know me, of course, I began to cry. I told them how passionate I was about Christian education and how it has always been my dream to become a teacher. I shared with them that I had indeed been out of school for a while and I just couldn't remember what cooperative learning was. I told them that if they hired me that I would not let them down. I would leave this interview and I would research the answer to that question and the next time if they should ask me what cooperative learning is, I would be able to tell them. With tears flowing from all three of our eyes, they said they had a few more interviews and they would let me know next week if I had the job.

Now you know how much torture this was for me. I heard through the grapevine, that the job was mine, but I couldn't be for sure. Finally, before I had to leave for my mission trip to Africa, I got a call from Miss Q, the principal, that I had indeed secured the position of the new first-grade teacher at Dupont Park SDA School in Washington, DC. I was jumping for joy and thanking God. While speaking to her on the phone, I told her that right after the interview I looked up cooperative learning, and I then told her what it was. She laughed and said she knew I would do my research, that's why she hired me. She said she loved my energy, enthusiasm, and passion for kids and knew that I'd make an excellent teacher. Now for those of you out there who are wondering what cooperative learning is, here is the definition: Cooperative learning is a successful teaching strategy in which small teams, each with students of different levels of ability, use a variety of learning activities to improve their understanding of a subject. I shall NEVER forget that, ever!

CHAPTER 2

Preparing to Take the Stage

Have you ever just got tired of teaching and doing the same ole' thing in the classroom? Do you want your students to remember everything you teach to them? Do you wish that you were more creative? Do you wish there was a book that could help you get that spark back in your teaching? Well, this book can help you. This book will give you some great ideas, awesome websites, resources, and a new outlook on your teaching style. It will help you get those creative juices flowing and even help you to communicate better with your student's parents. I have researched different websites, blogs, and stalked other teachers to find their best teaching strategies and merged them with mine. I have not created everything you see in this book, but I have made it my very own having added my twist on them. You can definitely do the same. This book will take you on a creative journey from August to May. Each month will highlight important dates and activities to go along with those days. I will help you to find ways to celebrate with your students. I will make it as plain as possible, so you can fully understand it. I may just leave out some of those "big educational words"...hehehe. Although I teach first grade, you can alter it for your grade level.

Before we begin, ask yourself, how can you set the stage for your students? Remember that your classroom is your stage. Did you prepare your lessons with individual students in mind? Are your lessons differentiated, or did you just make one lesson? What do you want your students to walk away with? What is the end goal? When you are planning your lessons, are they educational? Were you creative and thinking out of the box when planning? Can you hold their attention? Do your plans have rigor? And lastly, are your lessons fun and engaging? Let's gooooo!

As a teacher, I want my students to be lifelong learners. When I am creating my lesson plans and preparing to take the stage, I first have to recognize, understand, and know my students. Do you know who your students are? I am in constant communication with their teacher before me. I have their test scores and data, so I know a little about them academically before they enter the door. But I also want to know the type of learners they are. How they learn best? What excites them about learning? What does not excite them about learning? So, I give a quick assessment on learning styles to find out exactly what type of learner they are. Are they kinesthetic learners? Verbal? Auditory? This test helps me to better teach each student by knowing the type of learner they are.

With my students in mind, I want to make sure that my lessons align with the Common Core State Standards (CCSS) and that they are engaging and rigorous. The Common Core State Standards Initiative is an educational initiative in the United States that details what K–12 students should know in English language arts and mathematics at the end of each grade (Wikipedia). The states that have adopted CCSS routinely review their academic standards and may choose to change or add onto the standards to best meet the needs of their students. I live in Maryland, so my state follows CCSS. With this guideline, I am free to make up my own lessons, change the ones in the teacher's edition book, and be totally creative with my lessons as long as each of these standards are met by the end of the academic year.

With CCSS, my lessons don't have to go by the book word for word, which can be boring at times, ok all the time. The teacher's edition will always give you a basic outline to follow, but YOU must gear it to your students and make it teachable to your style. This again is preparation for taking the stage, which is your classroom. As a professional singer, I must take steps to ensure that on performance day, I will be ready. I may take vocal lessons, memorize a song, go to rehearsals, and even drink tea to help soothe my vocal cords. All in all, I am preparing for the big show. You may wonder what being a singer has to do with teaching? Well, for sure both must be prepared for and that's most important. With any profession, not just singing or teaching, one must always be prepared. You can't just get up in front of your audience (students) and wing it. Know the material, study it, and even practice it in a mirror if that'll help. Don't ever let your students see you unprepared.

I often find myself giving myself homework. Have you ever done that? There are times when a new curriculum is introduced, and I may not be familiar with the content. I take it home and familiarize myself with the information. I find ways to make it fun, engaging, and rigorous. Using the Teacher's Edition as a guide and resource is awesome but creating lessons with each student in mind can take your teaching to the next level. You have not only used your resources, but you have thought out how you can differentiate to meet the needs of all students. You have remembered that all students learn differently. What works for one student may not work for the next student. When I am thinking of the individual needs of my students, I get excited and the wheels start spinning on how I can make memorable lessons. Lessons that will go with them throughout a lifetime and they had fun while doing it. I am not saying that every lesson should have the students bouncing off the walls, but it should leave them remembering the lesson and asking questions about it. If your student can turn and talk, tell their peer what they learned, write it down, draw a picture, tell you about it, and complete an exit ticket, I would say, they have mastered that concept and you can move on to the next. Now let's find out how we can get them to this point.

CHAPTER 3

Rigor. What Is It?

used to have a problem when administrators would say, "you must teach with rigor." What is rigor? I was always so confused because I needed some concrete examples of rigor. Don't just tell me, show me, give me examples of what it really is. I found that Barbara R. Blackburn and Jacqui Murray are two educators who have made my understanding of rigor a reality. Rigor is defined as, "assignments that encourage students to think critically, creatively, and more flexibly." It requires students to question their assumptions and think deeply, rather than just lessons that merely demand memorization and information recall. A fill-in-the-blank worksheet would not be considered rigorous. Rigor is NOT lots of homework, projects, resources, or rules. When those four nouns are used to define rigor, the teacher is failing, not being creative, and thinking quantity is quality. That more is better. Absolutely not. Rigor is not about adding a column of data or remembering the main characters in a Shakespeare play. It's seeing how knowledge connects to life, to circumstances, and to daily problems (Murray, Jacqui). I have been researching the word rigor in education to get a better understanding of it. Murray said, Simply put, adding rigor creates an environment where students are:

- EXPECTED TO LEARN at high levels.
- SUPPORTED SO THEY CAN LEARN at high levels.
- CHEERED ON AS THEY DEMONSTRATE LEARNING at high levels.

I know with all that said, sometimes it's just not enough. I know I want and need to see examples of how this rigor can work in a classroom. I have found 22 examples of how to implement rigor in the classroom from Murray. I won't give them all, just the twelve that have helped me to become a better teacher. These are higher-order ways of thinking to help students excel.

1. Build GRIT in students. Let them know they are capable, competent, that thinking hard does not mean they didn't understand. It means they want to understand.

When students believe that they can learn, it is so much easier to teach them. I found that for students who have insecurities about school, their self-esteem, confidence, or behavior, it can be extremely hard to reach those students. I start the year by telling my students that they are Superstars. I tell them they will shine in their own special way. I explain to them that they are coming into my class with a clean slate. This new slate will allow them to learn new things and apply them all year. I have an actual slate. I hold it up with written unacceptable behaviors and I begin to wipe it clean. I tell them we are beginning again. This slate will free them from whatever they did last year behaviorally. There will always be those students who tell you how students behaved the previous year. I shut that down quickly. I let them know that I don't care about their behavior from last year. I tell them that they are smart, intelligent, that they'll become authors and illustrators in my class. I get them excited about learning and all of the possibilities first grade can bring. I let them know that if there are 27 students in the class, each one learns differently from the next student. I tell them not to compare their learning to other students learning. As a teacher, encourage them, let them know that they are capable and competent to take over the world. And that's the start of Superstar behavior.

2.   EXPECT INQUIRY. Be prepared. Make time for it.

When teaching a lesson, you always want your students to inquire about what you are teaching them. Asking questions is a big part of learning. If one never asks a question, how will one ever know the answer? No question is silly, wrong, or right. Sometimes, they will bring a totally different perspective and you must make time for it. Don't rush their process of thinking. Give them wait time to solve problems. Try to think ahead when planning your lesson for those out-of-the-box questions. Be sure to make them feel comfortable to ask those questions or inquire about what you just taught. Also, don't think that your point of view is always right. Allow students to disagree and or add on to what you asked or said. When you see a student thinking about the question you just asked or the statement you made, allow them to freely answer without interruptions.

3.   When you ASK A QUESTION, PAUSE. Let students think before answering. This wait time isn't delaying your lesson. In a rigorous classroom, it is the lesson.

Sometimes because of time restraints, you want to ask a question and rush the students to answer. You start pulling equity sticks, calling names trying to get a quick answer. Don't do that. After asking a question, pause and let the student ponder on the answer, ensuring that they have thought about it and want to give an accurate answer. Although you will have those students who raise their hands quickly to answer, still give wait time and then call on that student.

4.   FACE UNKNOWN QUESTIONS WITH A SMILE. Make the classroom a safe, non-judgmental learning environment where students can practice their critical thinking skills.

As a first-grade teacher, I have had students say some unexpected things. Whether it is talking about what happened at their house the night before, blurting out a phrase they heard on the radio or TV, or just saying the first thing that came to their minds that had absolutely nothing to do with what you were teaching...don't lose your cool. Keep a straight face and answer to the best of your ability. Never make them feel that you are judging what they said. Always make them feel comfortable talking to you and the class. Remember that this is a time in their lives where they are learning and exploring. Asking questions helps them practice their critical thinking skills...you want to encourage that by all means. Be sure to not embarrass them or make them feel like they said something wrong.

> Make the classroom a safe, non-judgmental learning environment where students can practice their critical thinking skills.

5. Focus on EXCEPTIONAL EXPECTATIONS.

Right off the back, students should know what the expectations of your classroom are. Mediocracy is not the key. I want my students to strive for excellence, so in all that I do, I set the example of how to be an exceptional Superstar. I am a mentor teacher, so I expect the students who I mentor to set high standards for their students. I work with these mentees and I lead by example. I come to school excited every day without coffee. I have adopted a slogan from a friend of mine ET the Hip Hop Preacher, "Thank God It's Monday". Be excited that you have another opportunity to instill greatness in your students another week. If I have a bad day, YOU WILL NOT KNOW. When planning lessons with the mentees, they see that I am looking for that first five minutes of excitement to get the students engaged. Bring out that prior knowledge, something to trigger their minds. When you set the standards high for your students, they will follow. It will be all they know. Don't take anything less. Set the standard high and they will exceed your expectations.

6. As students participate in class conversations, EXPECT THEM TO USE ACADEMIC AND DOMAIN-SPECIFIC VOCABULARY. If they use words like "something," "you know," "that," or "like," prod them to come up with specifics. "Like what? No, I don't know." This immerses them in learning, discovering, and thinking critically.

This is important. Using the vocabulary that is directly related to the subject matter ensures that the student is thinking critically. An example can be with introducing a new math lesson. Each lesson gives vocabulary words. Introduce those words and be sure that YOU as a teacher are using the vocabulary, don't just expect it from them. Remember you are modeling the behavior you want to see them exhibit. Post these vocabulary words in the room on anchor charts. When it is time for a student to answer a question, prod them to use specific vocabulary when answering the question.

7. As students answer questions, EXPECT EVIDENCE TO SUPPORT THEIR ANSWERS. This can come from personal experience, but more often will find relevance from learning resources.

Using evidence when students discuss a text or learned information builds and strengthens their confidence and comprehension. A student who can cite evidence in a given text assignment shows the teacher that they have actually done their work. Classroom discussions are the perfect time to let the students lead. After reading, they can quote, know pages, and prove that their answers are correct.

8. LISTEN TO STUDENT ANSWERS. Pay attention. Challenge them to be thorough.

That's right! Listen to your students' answers. Let them know that you are very interested in what they have to say. How would you feel if someone asked you a question and you had the perfect answer, but they began to look at their phone before/while you were answering? If a student raises their hand to answer a question, they thought about it and had the courage to raise their hand. Give them the respect to listen, even if it is way off. Let them know that every word that comes out of their mouth is important. Ask them questions to help them to become thorough in their answers. No one-word answers. Repeat the question and then answer so everyone knows exactly what you mean.

9. DON'T DRAW CONCLUSIONS FOR STUDENTS. Present them with evidence. See where it takes them.

Now, this can be a hard one to accomplish, but you have to be conscious not to give your students the answer. Sometimes, it's hard not to probe the little ones, but don't do it. Always give them the evidence and see where it will take them. When you let a child use their own brain or their imagination, instead of giving your two cents, they are more likely to become independent, critical thinkers, and problem solvers. Giving the answer provides a crutch that they will always search for in the classroom and it can carry on throughout their lives. We don't want that! I want my students to be able to see or hear the evidence and go from there.

10. SUPPORT STUDENTS, so they can reach high expectations. If they are thinking outside the box, don't pull them back in. Ask questions: Is this approach going to meet expectations, solve problems, achieve desired results? If it is, let them do it!

When a student has the support of the teacher, they are confident. A teacher must always support their students with questions to be sure that they are using and reaching the desired expectations. Do this without your opinion, but with support. This again provides an opportunity for independent and critical thinking for the student. Thinking outside the box is one way to solve problems, but your job as a teacher is to push students and support their thinking. Supporting their thinking allows the student to think about questions and answers they never would have thought about.

11. Provide a way for each student to DEMONSTRATE LEARNING even if it isn't a way you've thought of. Applaud them if they devise an approach that works for them.

> You are doing your job if you ask a student to explain a concept you just taught them and they turn that thing around and surprise you with an answer that is totally out of the box, but on point.

Don't get salty if your students can take a concept that you've taught them and work it out differently. The goal is to help students be more independent, create problem solvers and critical thinkers. You are doing your job if you ask a student to explain a concept you just taught them and they turn that thing around and surprise you with an answer that is totally out of the box but on point. Mannnnn, your chest should be stuck waaay out! I love Whole-Brain teaching and I implement, "turn and talk" in my class. This is when students turn to each other and teach the concept you just taught them to each other. I walk around and listen to what they are saying to be sure they are on track. One time, to my surprise a student took what I said and gave it a whole new face. It made so much sense, that I told the class that I thought that this student had a better way to explain what I just said. I had that student come up in front of the class and teach the entire class his way. Ohhh! You should have seen his big smile. I applauded his way and that made his day. It made the other students think harder and longer and they all came up with different ways and ideas to master the concept. Although they wanted that praise and recognition from me, it was just what I wanted to happen. Hey, by any means necessary to reach the ideal goal. Awesome, yep, totally awesome!

12. **DIFFERENTIATE FOR STUDENT NEEDS. If you have a project that seems to fit everyone, it doesn't. How do I know that? Because no project does.**

No two students are alike. "Designed differentiation is the deliberate act of modifying instruction or an assignment in order to customize the effect to match the particular developmental level and skills of a student or group of students. The ideal is to provide equivalent learning activities that cater to the students' strengths but bring all of the students to the same learning objective" (Johnson, Ben). Using the CCSS comes in handy when differentiating. You can find the standard and modify it for your students by looking at the grade above or grade below to create lessons. The end will bring students to the same learning goal but on a different level.

When planning lessons, you may want to take the easy road and plan just one lesson. This will not work. Every lesson will not fit all. Some learners are hands-on (physical/kinesthetic), some learners need to see concrete resources to help them (visual/spatial), some learners have to move and make up songs to recall (aural/auditory/musical), that's me, and some learners can just take what you say and run with it (verbal/linguistic). There are many different types of learners, so plan your lessons for the individual student. You may have different groups of students, so within those groups try to differentiate. You must do this with homework as well. I take time to think of each student and what they need, and I often have four different sets of homework if necessary. The goal is to reach every student no matter what level they are on. It is tasking, I must admit, but you want to be sure that each scholar is getting what they need from you. I feel that providing students with the work they need makes them feel safe, loved, and smart. I have had parents who have struggling students complete their homework without their help at night. It's because I want each student to feel smart and to be able to do work on their levels. Homework is just a mirror of what was taught in the classroom, so it should be simple to do each night, not taking forever to get it done. Students like to feel independent and know that they can complete homework without any assistance. Differentiation can save your life as a teacher and a student. Provide that student with homework that is not like the others, but something they can stick their chest out about. Reaching a student where they are and seeing them master a task on their level is key. Of course, you are challenging them along the way, but mastery is the goal.

I hope that by using these 12 higher-order ways to implement rigor, your classroom and students will walk away with knowledge for a lifetime. It may take your students out of their comfort zones, but making lifelong learners is key. Superstar status can be reached. It will prepare them to solve problems they will face in the future and not be afraid to tackle them. That's what a rigorous classroom can do! As a parent, you never want your child to take the easy way out. You want them to walk, but you don't want to hold their hands all the time. You want them to be independent to run and explore. You want them to grow and experience life with all that the world has to offer them. You don't want everything handed to them on a platter because they will never know how to live and work in the real world. You should want the same thing for your students. You want to teach them the necessary skills, but then you want to see them use them without your help.

CHAPTER 4

Beginning the School Year

What are you doing as a teacher? Do you have energy when you enter the class? Do you come to class unhappy about something that happened at home? Don't burden your students with that. Be cheerful! Be happy! Be excited about what the day has to offer! Never let them know that you are having a bad day. You are about to take the stage inside your classroom. Your audience is your bright-eyed, eager-to-learn students. You have rehearsed, I mean prepared your lessons... You have dressed appropriately, your smile is ear to ear, and your inner Superstar is about to appear.

A successful day consists of a teacher who has planned for his/her students. You have thought out exactly how you want the lesson to go and are ready and excited to present it to your students. Tell them to put their thinking caps on or their investigative glasses...you can tell, I teach the little ones...LOL! But it actually works for older students as well. It's time to be a Superstar learner.

I don't know where my energy comes from, but my students are worn out when they leave my class. I have pictures from parents to prove it. Ok, I do know where my energy comes from. It comes from knowing that my students will learn something new. It comes from knowing that I have created a lesson that is exciting, fun, and invigorating. It comes from seeing their eyes pop open with excitement because they understand and know what I am teaching about. I have worked their brains and worked off some of their energy. I have taught them songs, chants, dances, we have marched, stomped, and cheered to make sure that each concept has been mastered. And again, you can do this with your older students, of course, modified a bit. They like to have fun, too. Like I said, I've gotten texts from parents with pictures of their kids in the car on the ride home knocked out with the question, "What did y'all do today?" I don't drink coffee, I occasionally have chai tea, but I'm a morning person and I wake up that way. I can keep up that energy throughout the day because I know that my students are learning and if I don't, they'll be bored and unengaged.

I watch the energy of my brother ET the Hip Hop Preacher, he's always on. I often look for that off switch, but there is none. He is motivated by the lives he can change each day and what he can do for his family. I read about and watch videos of Ron Clark and his staff, they all have that energy that is exuded to their students and audiences. They have passion and I have it, too. Do you? Just thinking about how I can impact the lives of students brings tears to my eyes. I am given a blank slate and have the privilege to impart wisdom to them. It all just makes me beam from the inside.

Start your day off right. Listen to music, a motivational speaker, or whatever you have to do before you get up in front of your class. You CANNOT get up in front of a class unprepared and expect your students to just get it. This is your stage, your platform to impart knowledge to young minds. Think about a Superstar. Does that person just take the stage to act or sing? Absolutely NOT!! They are in front of a mirror rehearsing those monologues, they are in a rehearsal hall practicing with the band, the choreographer, and with the vocal coach. They want their performances to be seamless. I refer to my students as Superstars. Superstars are prepared, they have worked hard, and they are now famous because of it. It didn't just happen overnight. I want that same thing for my students, but in the classroom. Be prepared. Create Superstar lessons. Make it fun, interesting, and challenging. Start off with a bang each day. Your students will thank you for it.

As a teacher, I am always looking for lessons that will engage my students. I want lifelong learners, and by engaging them, I know that they will recall information easily. "If you just tell your students, they will forget. If you teach them, they will remember. But if you involve them, they will learn" (Benjamin Franklin). So, I sit and plan lessons with each student in mind. I want

> "If you just tell your students, they will forget. If you teach them, they will remember. But if you involve them, they will learn."
>
> – Benjamin Franklin

to reach each one, get them involved, so I'm sure to create lessons that they can relate to. I search the internet. I follow other teachers on Instagram. I have a TeachersPayTeachers account and I purchase lessons that I think my students would like. I don't always reinvent the wheel. If it is there and something that I can use, I buy it, use it, and make it my own. Your delivery is what makes it yours.

My students always like to hear stories from when I was a kid. So, I start out telling you something about me, how I learned to do a certain task or lesson. It intrigues them and they then try to apply what I said I do/did and do it in their own way. It's magic and it works. You are the reason a child wants to learn. In the first five minutes of introducing the lesson, wow them and get their creative juices flowing. Believe me, it's their motivation. They love when they can relate to something you are saying. You'll see the hands go flying up.

Now that we have learned all about me, Common Core State Standards, and rigor, it's time to find out what I do during the year to make a memorable year. The school year is 10 months long. That's a lot of teaching going on...180 days to be exact. Every lesson can't include backflips, but there can be a few that will WOW them. Let's start with the month of August. Most schools start after Labor Day, but because I teach at a private school, school starts the second week of August. So I usually have two good weeks left in the month to work with.

CHAPTER 5

August

Important Dates

AUGUST 1 — *Francis Scott Key's Birthday*

AUGUST 5 — *Watermelon Day*

AUGUST 11 — *Night of the Shooting Stars*

AUGUST 14 — *Victory Day*

AUGUST 19 — *Aviation Day*

AUGUST 28 — *"I Have a Dream" Day*

Monthly Themes

Clean Water Month

Smile Week – *Second week*

Friendship Day – *First Sunday*

August: WOW Them!!

I teach at a small private school. My principal gives me the opportunity to come up with a theme for the entire school year. So, before school lets out, I am already thinking of what we can do for the next year that will be more exciting than the current year. I do my research and try to find something that will be totally exciting for the students. After I have about 3 themes, I call up my team during the summer, yes, the summer, to run a few ideas by them. I never want to just come up with it on my own. Five heads are better than one! It's a blessing when you have co-workers who you can depend on and who are team players, even in the summer. The theme that we come up with must WOW the students and the parents. It has to have all of the elements to bring excitement on the first day of school.

The first day of school is VERY important. When the students and parents walk into the building on the first day of school, you want them to be WOWED! You want to hear all the ooooh's and ahhhh's. First impressions are lasting impressions. It must be a day that everyone remembers and talks about. How can you do this? Get a committee together and put your brilliant minds together. Discuss how you want the day to go and make a plan for execution. All teachers must be on board to see the plan through. All ideas are accepted and then narrowed down to the best ones. The first day of school MUST be spectacular!!

The weeks before school begins start preparing the school. Think about what you want the hallways to look like, what are the classrooms going to look like? What will the students see when they first enter the building? The theme should be shown throughout the school. Whatever door the students enter, they should be welcomed with open arms. The teachers should be standing there with smiles on their faces. It should be bright and colorful. Prepare the entry with balloons and give them something to remind them of the first day. Having a supportive team is key. It must be a day that everyone remembers and talks about. Here are four themes that our school has done. Of course, I searched the web for ideas, but then, you make them your own. Simple, right? Yes! Let's get into it.

Cooking Up a Great School Year

Cooking Up a Great School year is just what it says... keyword, cooking. Each month, we cooked. Each teacher should choose a recipe or assign one to teach to the students once a month at assembly. In my class, whether it was pizza, soup, pancakes, or cookies, we did it. These recipes were integrated into our lessons. We learned about other countries and the different types of foods they eat. We made up recipes, measured, got dirty, and executed the recipes. The great thing about school-wide themes is that they are carried out throughout the year in my classroom. So, it is little to no thought on what can be accomplished when there is already a theme in place. Get those creative juices flowing, search the internet, and make your lessons memorable.

On the first day of school, each teacher was given an apron that said, "Cooking Up a Great School Year" and a chef's hat. Of course, our school is always on a budget, but there are ways you can get around that. Make it yourself!! That's what I did. I bought inexpensive plain white aprons off the internet. I found a great picture that I liked and sent it to a friend of mine who then put the words on the picture for me. I went to Michael's and bought a pack of iron-on film. I put the film through the printer and sent the picture to print. There you have it, an iron-on picture. I simply ironed the picture onto the apron and it was awesome. No one would have ever known that I actually made them. I was very proud of them!

There were banners that read "Cooking Up a Great School Year". I got them made at Staples. I always look for a bargain...so I talked the guy behind the counter down on the price. I went on to tell him how I was a poor teacher living on a budget, we are, right? And it worked...LOL! That morning on the first day of school, we made pancakes and gave juice to every student and parent who walked through the door. We had colorful balloons and welcomed each one with hugs and or a handshake. We were loudly welcoming everyone back. Parents were thrilled to see such an awesome first day and felt comfortable leaving their kids in our hands. The students were excited to be back and the new students felt at home and welcomed. It was truly a day to remember.

T.E.A.M. Players
(Together Everyone Achieves More)

The theme T.E.A.M. Players was developed because our team at school is one of a kind. Do you have a TEAM that you look forward to working with? We love to help each other in whatever ways we can. We decided that this year we would work as a TEAM and give the students examples of TEAMWORK. So often, students are self-centered and think that the world revolves around them. They think that they can do everything by themselves, even down to winning a basketball game. So, we wanted to teach students that if they can work together as a team they can achieve more. We wanted them to see us as teachers working together without fussing or fighting. And I tell you no lie, the teachers at my school never fuss or fight. We can almost always come to an agreement. And that's truly a blessing when you work with like-minded teachers.

To begin, each teacher chose a sport to complete their bulletin boards in the hallways and classroom. We chose sports because, with sports, there are teams. These teams have to work together to win. They have to depend and count on one another. Each board had its own title to go along with its sport. We had T-shirts made for the first day of school. Every teacher, staff member, and administrator wore the TEAM shirt to represent our great TEAM. We had a Red Carpet with balloons. Teachers lined the red carpet and welcomed each student. We had a photographer who snapped pictures as each child came in. We gave the students popcorn and pencils as a goodie gift.

We yelled, welcome back to school as each student walked through the door. They were giving out hugs as well. It was certainly another day to remember.

In my class, I took this theme a bit further and focused on all things TEAM each month. We started off with our class as a TEAM and how we could make our "Class TEAM" work for the year. We worked on TEAMWORK for the duration of August, being sure to implement classroom rules, hallway rules, friend rules, and how each of us play an important part in class to make it work. Then each month a new sport, a choir, a family, whatever exemplified a TEAM was introduced and we learned about it and how each member of the TEAM is valuable. There is no "I" in TEAM, so they must work together to WIN!

Speaking of classroom rules, how do you manage your class? Here's what I do.

Classroom Management

Like I mentioned before, my school starts in August, but whenever your school begins, you can start. This is the month when you get to know the students, their individual learning styles, and personalities and they get to learn all about you. Classroom management is key. Classroom management creates a set of expectations used in the classroom. In an organized classroom, there are rules, routines, and consequences. This is the time to set high standards and expectations for your students. This is when I introduce how to become a Superstar.

Effective classroom management sets the stage for teachers to engage students in effective learning. Imagine a classroom without rules or routines. Oh my! How do you say mayhem? The students can get off-task, cause major disruptions, and the teacher has to constantly redirect behavior. There will be no teaching and learning (as my principal gingerly says) in a classroom without classroom management.

Classroom rules are established in the beginning of the year and this is the time you tell your students what you expect of them. Set the bar high. Begin to put those rules in place, constantly go over the routines and any procedures you want your class to follow. If you want your classroom environment to run smoothly, consistency is key. Stick with what you start with. When students know where to put homework, where to line up, how to line up, or how to transition to centers or the next subject, it makes your life easier. You will not have to spend time giving directions and wasting precious instructional time.

One year, I thought I spent enough time on routines and rules in my class, but I clearly didn't. My students followed for a little while but ended up going in the opposite direction of where I wanted them to be. I spent more time that year giving directions and reiterating what was expected of them. Imagine my day! I tell you; I tried several different ways to implement the rules and expectations of my classroom and nothing seemed to work. Soooo, frustrating. So, when you think that you have spent enough time on routines and classroom management, YOU HAVEN'T. Keep implementing your rules and routines until it becomes natural for the students. When you are consistent, your students will be consistent.

Again, stick to your initial rules. Changing what you started can make the students think that you do not know what you are doing. Don't ever let that happen, my friend. I say, think about your students with the end in mind. Think about how you want your students to behave when you are absent and need a substitute. Once your classroom rules have been embedded in their little brains, you can count on your class to follow through and be the Superstars you know they can be. You'll be surprised at how your students can run your classroom when you are not there. But you'll be pleasantly surprised when the substitute gives you a good report. And boy oh boy, a smile will be plastered on your face!

I have researched the best classroom management habits for students. Classroom management does not only deal with behavior, but this management creates an entire classroom environment. There are so many great ones out there, but you must choose the ones that can make your classroom successful. The book *Teach Like a Champion* by Doug Lemov offers 49 techniques that can help you to teach smarter and manage your classroom. I fought hard to not use some of these, but our Curriculum Coordinator insisted that these techniques can make for a better classroom environment... she was right! These techniques also claim to help put students on the path to college. I can see how it can be effective. I will not list all 49, but I will list the subtitles. You can get this book or look it up online. Here they are:

- Setting high academic expectations
- Planning that ensures academic achievement
- Structuring and delivering your lessons
- Engaging students in your lessons
- Creating a strong classroom culture
- Setting and maintaining high behavioral expectations
- Building character and trust
- Improving your pacing
- Challenging students to think critically

Check this book out when you get a chance. It's a great resource. There is also a *Teach Like a Champion 2.0.* This book gives 62 techniques.

Whole Brain Teaching

Another proven management style is Whole Brain Teaching, it has awesome classroom management strategies, too. I have adopted most of the rules for my classroom. Whole Brain Teaching focuses on "teaching challenging students" by catching your class's attention early on and holding it by creating a positive classroom environment that is both fun and educational, fostering both academic and social-emotional growth in your students (Maldonado, Stephan). Whole Brain Techniques were designed by a college educator Chris Biffle, a kindergarten instructor Jay Vanderfin, and a 4th-grade teacher

Chris Rekstad. These three educators set out to create a "radical new teaching system" that was "brain-based", fun, and free (Maldonado). There are various YouTube videos to help a teacher who is trying to adopt Whole Brain Teaching. I like the enthusiasm, talkback, mimicking, chants, and responses of these strategies. Just like Teach Like a Champion has various methods, so does Whole Brain Teaching. There are 7. Of the 7, I use 5 of them daily. Here are the 7.

Step 1: Class-Yes.

This is the attention-getter to begin every class. The teacher says, "class" in any voice he/she chooses, and the class mimics the teacher in the same voice by responding yes.

Step 2: Classroom Rules

- Follow directions quickly
- Raise your hand for permission to speak
- Raise your hand for permission to leave your seat
- Make smart choices
- Keep your dear teacher happy (my favorite)

All of these rules are repeated before lessons each day, several times a day to ensure all students understand the rules. The rules are also done with hand motions. So cute. I love them. You can find these rules online and print them out. These rules are printed out and placed on my whiteboard. Just in case your students forget what each rule is, they can take a quick lookup and find them.

Step 3: Teach-OK.

Students are divided into two groups 1's and 2's, each student will rotate. Students listen to the instruction of the teacher, turn and teach each other when the teacher says teach, they say teach OK.

Again, if this seems a bit confusing, there are many YouTube videos with these methods being done. You can find one on my YouTube channel Forever First Grade.

Step 4: Scoreboard Game.

Depending on the grade, students are given smileys, frowns, or points. They are added up and then celebrated or redirected.

Step 5: Hands and Eyes.

I love this attention-getter. The teacher says hands and eyes, and students mimic hands and eyes. Whatever students are doing, they stop and fold their hands, and all eyes are on the teacher.

Step 6: Mirror.

Very similar to hands and eyes. The mirror allows the teacher to gain control of the classroom with students mimicking her motions and voice.

Step 7: Switch.

Use this step with "Teach-OK". Be sure that while students are teaching, that the same student is not used all the time. Say switch, and students will say switch and the groups will rotate. Of the seven, I use numbers 1, 2, 3, and 5. Kudos to these educators.

I love the Whole Brain teaching methods. I use these steps in my class daily, along with some other practices I have found to manage my classroom. In everything that you do with your students, be consistent. Stick with whatever you started with your students. These simple rules are everything. Practice, practice, and practice these rules until they become habits to the students. It makes for a much smoother year and managing your classroom.

Around The World In 180 Days

I love to travel, and I have been to a lot of beautiful countries. I searched the web and found that this was a theme in several schools. But to make ours special, I wanted it to be an interactive project where the students could learn about different countries. Of course, I thought it out and met with my summer team to present it to them. They loved the idea!! So my wheels began to turn. How can this year of 180 Days Around the World be spectacular? I emailed the entire staff and told them what I had come up with and asked if they had any ideas that they can add to it. I asked them to choose a country that they'd like to present to the students. Of course, the teachers chose the country where they are from. We represent so many wonderful countries and I couldn't wait to learn about them, especially if I have never been there. So, each teacher chose their country and the rest is history.

When traveling to other countries, you must have a passport, so I decided that I would try and find a passport to give to each student. Of course, they were too expensive, so I had them made. On each page of the passport were the countries that the teachers chose for the 10 months of school. Each teacher had to come up with 5-6 facts or things they thought were important about that country. So when they presented the country, these facts had to be included. These facts were also included on the passport page for the students. We made a stamp with the theme on it. When a specific country was presented and the students were able to answer the questions, their passports were stamped. So exciting to get all of the stamps for learning about each country. So, even if a student has never been to these particular countries, they can now say, they learned all about it. And one day, they may decide to visit these countries.

To begin, each teacher created bulletin boards to represent their countries. So the hallways coincided with the theme. We purchased flag banners of different countries to hang down the hallways as well. There was even a USA bulletin board and the students had to stop there to pick up their passports. The foyer of the school also had a themed bulletin board with a world on it and 180 days Around the World. There were flags representing each country hanging above the board. The school was looking great!!! We were now ready for the new school year.

On the first day of school, each teacher dressed in the attire

from their chosen country. The countries represented were Tanzania, Russia, Canada, Korea, Ghana, India, and so many more. They were beautiful. We had a Red Carpet once again to welcome the students with balloons. Each student received a key ring with a world on it and a pencil with different flags to represent the countries as they walked through the door. They were greeted by the principal and vice-principal who were also dressed in their chosen countries. It was truly a day to remember. I am sure you can achieve this at your school.

Each month, when it was time to present their chosen country at assembly, the teachers did phenomenal jobs!!! OH MY!!! The things they came up with were excellent. The teachers put thought and effort into each presentation and even provided food from their countries.

My favorite was the Caribbean (Jamaica). This teacher provided an array of Jamaican delights. She invited a band and someone was playing the steel pans.

The students enjoyed attending the assembly once a month to learn about different countries and they also received great treats. The memory of each country is embedded in their minds. A student told me after I presented the country of Tanzania, that she wanted to be just like me and go to Tanzania and be a missionary. I told the

story of how I was chosen to go with my mother who would be the housemother to orphans there. I went there to help build a house for them. My job as an educator was to create a classroom in the house. I immediately turned to my friends and asked for help because I knew I wouldn't be able to afford all of the supplies for this classroom. I have the best friends, because before I knew it, crayons, books, paper, glue, pencils, you name it, started coming in. We had decorations for bulletin boards, letters, stencils, etc. to make this room a classroom where the children would love to come but hate to leave. I gave it 200% and the classroom was top-notch. I dressed the part, told the story through pictures, and students have not forgotten it. One day, they'll be able to go on a mission trip to Tanzania and help orphans as I did. Making lasting impressions and lifelong learners.

A school must have willing teachers who are excited and really love what they do. Are you a passionate teacher, or did you just take this job because it was easy to get a degree? Becoming a teacher was a no-brainer for me. It is all that I dreamed of as a little girl. I love being a teacher! I always wanted to go the extra mile, even if it costs to make it a reality. When students can actually see that you are excited about teaching and learning, it sets a standard for them. They too want to be innovative, creative, and successful. You must be the example you want them

> When students can actually see that you are excited about teaching and learning, it sets a standard for them.

to be. Show them that you are passionate about teaching, that you care enough to make learning extra special. They'll never forget you or what they've learned from you, just like I have never forgotten my teachers and all that they instilled in me. Coming from a single-parent home, poor, and on welfare, I had loving, thoughtful, kind, and passionate teachers who cared about me and my education. Those impressions are embedded in my head forever.

Oh geez, that came from nowhere. So back to the first day of school. When you are trying to decide on your theme, remember to include your teammates, although you are the one heading the project. A successful team creates successful work. You don't have to carry the theme throughout the year, but it can be wonderful if you did. Most importantly, be sure that the first day of school is one the students will always remember, and say WOW that was the best first day ever.

Dive Into Reading

Somehow reading has become obsolete. Students would rather watch TV, play video games, or do anything else but read. I love to read. Reading can take you on a journey when you let your imagination lead the way. Our school has done some amazing school year themes, but this one is very special. We wanted to make this theme extra special and make reading popular again. Our goal was to have students walking around the school reading. Reading in line, reading at lunch, and even reading on the playground. We wanted their heads buried in books. We set a goal of 5,000 books for the year. So, then we began to get the school ready for the first day of school.

In my class, one of my favorite projects to see my students present is the Brown Bag Project. This assignment is so exciting and fun for the students because they get to choose their favorite book and present it in an extra special, fun way. They get to dress up as a character in the book. Not only do they dress up as their favorite character, but they must also choose five items to represent a part in the book and put it in the bag. O.M.G....these kids are sooo adorable all dressed up as Fly Guy, as a baseball player, or a princess. Their parents go all out.

So, my idea was to have the teachers choose their favorite book, dress as their favorite character, and decorate their bulletin boards with items from their chosen book. Everyone was excited about it and we got started on it right away to make the first day for the students exciting. We knew the students would try guessing who each teacher was. It's always so awesome when you have teachers who are just as excited as you are about a theme. I always brag about the faculty and staff at my school because I get 100% participation from them all the time. Ok, well, I got 99% this time because we had a "cool" principal and he said he needed to be in a suit to greet new parents. I must admit that on other first days of school, he did oblige. I'll just let you know that the teachers went all out on their outfits and so did I. I was Junie B. Jones, yes, pigtails, glasses, striped leggins' and all. The students were very excited when they walked through the

door and onto the red carpet. Some are shy at first if they are new to the school, but the others high five and give hugs to each of the teachers. We let them know we are glad they are back. The parents snap pictures of this moment and are proud to see the teachers so involved. It kind of gives them a perspective of what they can expect throughout the year.

As the students are dismissed by grades, everyone walks down the hallway. The hallways are decorated, and the bulletin boards have the teacher's favorite book on them. So, if they didn't guess who the teachers were, they could look at their bulletin boards and figure it out. The excitement is still very high. I decided to go live on Facebook, so everyone could see our first day of school. It was awesome!

On back-to-school night, we told the parents what our goal was for reading. We gave each student a reading log to log each book that they read. Every Friday, students would turn in their logs. The teachers would keep track of the books and tally them at the end of the month. By the second month of school, the students had read more than 3,000 books. The class that read the most books, would receive a special treat like an ice cream party, pizza party, a movie, lunch with the principal, or something fun. The 1st place class was Mrs. Guerrero's Kindergarten class who read over 1,000 books. Kudos to them! I am now certain that our goal of 5,000 books for the year will have to be increased. These kids are knocking these books out of the park!

Whatever you decide to do on the first day of school or in choosing a theme for your school, stick with it. Get your students excited about whatever it is. Be excited about it yourself. Be sure that everyone is on board. Make this day one that students and parents alike will be talking about. I think that within the first two months, we had accomplished a few of our goals. We saw students walking around with books in their hands. They were reading at lunchtime, they were reading in the dismissal lines, and they were on the playground reading. I say that's a win-win for all.

CHAPTER 6

September

Important Dates

SEPTEMBER 1   **National Freedom Day**

SEPTEMBER 14   **National Anthem Day**

SEPTEMBER 15   **Hispanic Heritage Month Begins**

SEPTEMBER 16   **Mexico Independence Day**

SEPTEMBER 26   **Johnny Appleseed's Birthday**

SEPTEMBER 28   **Confucius' Birthday**

Monthly Themes

Labor Day – *First Monday*

Grandparents Day – *First Sunday after Labor Day*

Rash Hashanah
– First and Second day of the Jewish month of Tishri

American Indian Day – Fourth Friday

Cherokee National Holiday – Labor Day Weekend

While the month of September rolls up on you so quickly, you have to be prepared and ready to begin the month with a bang. You are still implementing your classroom rules and anything you deem necessary for your students. I am sure you already have your themes in place and can go from there.

From the beginning of the year, I like to focus on how we can work together as a class while implementing Superstar behavior. We will be together for 180 days and we must learn to get along as a family would. I tell them that they are brothers and sisters and while in class, I'm their mom...true, right? They slip up so many times and call me mom anyways. But we must work together to make our class a place of safety and they must know how they can be a team to make our class thrive. So, we begin with one of many books about teamwork.

T.E.A.M. Work: Stone Soup

In August, the first weeks of school, it is important to establish classroom rules. Without rules in a classroom, students can present behavior problems in the very beginning. When the school-wide theme was T.E.A.M. (Together Everyone Achieves More), our class worked together to find out how TEAMS are made. Who are the members of the TEAM? Why does it take more than one person to be on TEAM?

I give examples of the different types of teams I am on, and why I am important to those teams. I listed family, Virtue, a singing group, and a classroom team. There were oooohhh's and ahhh's when I wrote classroom that is a part of a team. One student raised his hand and said, I've never been on a team, but now I am. I'm on a classroom team. I said yes! Then I asked him, what could he do to make our classroom teamwork? He said I can share. I said AWESOME, that's the perfect answer. Then students started raising their hands to add to the list I was writing on the board.

We went through several teams, such as basketball, football, and choir. I used Lebron James as an example and asked them why they thought he made the Cav's basketball team work. Could he win championships all by himself? Absolutely, not! I then read them a story called Stone Soup. This story was about a village that was hungry, but no one had enough food to make a meal, only stones. So, this little boy in the village started going to each house to find out what each family could contribute to this meal. They all meet in the courtyard to put their items together. One family had potatoes, one had onions, meat, corn, and everyone gave to make the perfect soup because everyone was hungry. The moral of the story is that one person could not make a great soup with one ingredient. They began to tell how nasty it would taste if it only had onions and stones.

The day before I asked each student to bring in a vegetable. They didn't realize we were actually going to make Stone Soup in the classroom. This is one of the stories I brought to life. We acted out the entire story. They remembered each of the story parts and did a great job retelling it. This would be one of the many celebrations we would have in our class. I pulled out my Insta-Pot and we had yummy Stone Soup in 30 minutes, minus the stones, LOL. The students loved it. Each student contributed to the delicious soup. They all understood the moral of the story, that it takes more than one person to make a class, football team, or choir function. There is no "I" in TEAM, it can't be done alone. One lesson under the belts of The First Grade Superstars. And best of all, they had a yummy bowl of soup and will never forget how to be a part of a team.

Garden Party

I get excited when I know I have something extra special for the kids. I know it will be a treat when I think of it and tears swell in my eyes. Yep, the tears. I'm such a wuss. When I am planning a lesson and considering how we will celebrate in the end, I make sure that every student has mastered the concept. That means, they can tell me all about it, turn and talk to their peers about it, they can write about it, draw a picture, and finally complete an exit ticket.

I teach in a Christian institution, so we can pray and talk about our Creator whenever we want to. We pray to begin our day; we pray when there is a problem, and we have prayer requests for our loved ones. We just pray because we are thankful. At an early age, we want total dependence upon God. They know that they can go to Him anytime. I am not sure what you do in your school, but I am sure you can meditate, take a moment of silence, or do whatever it is to start your day.

Bible is an important subject at our school. Our first Bible lessons are about Creation, Adam and Eve, and living in the Garden of Eden. We learn how the world was created in 6 days, how Adam and Eve came about, and how they had the best home in the Garden of Eden with the animals, fruits, and veggies, and just living off of the land God created for them. Sounds like they were vegans to me. I make sure I add science in for cross-curricular learning about healthy choices and creation. My students learn how to choose an apple over a bag of salty greasy chips. God created our bodies in such a way that we can survive on the fruits, vegetables, nuts, and the grains of the earth. After the students truly understand and can talk about it, write about it, or draw a picture, and then it is time to celebrate.

For a week we chart their favorite types of fruit and comparing them to unhealthy foods such as chips, cookies, or soda on an anchor chart. I make a list on the board of every fruit and vegetable I can think of. I then tell the students; we will have a Garden Party to celebrate all of the fruits and vegetables that were created just for us. Hearing the word "celebrate" brings excitement to the students. Each student chooses a fruit to bring to the celebration.

On the day of the celebration, I cut all the fruit and veggies. Note: ask parents to send in the fruit already cut, it saves so much time. I bring in beautiful platters and arrange the fruit banquet style. When the students come back into the room from recess, they walk into a beautiful room full of fruit and veggies. The aroma alone makes them hungry. They are ready to partake in all that God has made for them. One time, I took all of the desks out of the classroom and we pretended we were in the Garden eating under my apple tree in the class. In the Garden of Eden, there was a forbidden fruit. I made one that the students aren't allowed to touch. I make it pretty tempting by adding shiny stars to a delicious red apple.

They learn the lessons of obedience and self-control by not touching them. A lesson all in itself. What a wonderful celebration. Oh, and parents will thank you because their child came home and had a great time in the bathroom...I know TMI! LOL!

The Adventures of Tilly

Also in the month of September, we are learning to write and spell. We are in the beginning stages of learning to take care of ourselves and others. I always wanted to have a classroom pet that the students can take home on the weekend and care for. I wanted them to write about their adventures of the weekend with the classroom pet. But that never happened. The closest I got to have a pet was beta fish. They lasted a while, then they would die. We'd have to plan a funeral and who wants that. Sooooo, this is how The Adventures of Tilly began.

When I was a schoolgirl, I loved to write. I would ask my mom to buy me notebooks, journals, paper, or whatever I could write on. I kept a diary or journal about everything that happened in my life. If I went to the store, I'd write about it. If I liked a boy or watched my favorite TV show, it could be found in my books. When I was happy or sad, or bored, you could find me writing in a corner somewhere. If my sisters made me upset, I'd go venting to my diary. Ok, ok, so, you get the gist of how much I love to write. I still have some of those journals to this day and I still go to my closet to write. It is amazing to look back and see how my handwriting has changed, how my thought process changed, and how even my vocabulary has developed. The writing was everything to me...even down to buying the perfect purple or blue pen to write with.

Somehow writing has lost its fervor. Computers, iPads, and smartphones have taken over and handwriting is a thing of the past. But I don't want this to happen to my students. I want them to find a love for writing. I want them to become excited about which pen to choose, finding that perfect journal or diary to write in. Expressing their feelings on paper and smiling as they are doing it.

So I bought Tilly as a pet for the classroom. Then I got this brilliant idea to have the students take him home on the weekends. I'm sure I could have seen this somewhere...LOL, but taking him home on the weekend would require some serious work on their part. Whoever got to take Tilly home, had to take him everywhere they went and then write about their adventures with him. This was going to be an exciting journey for the year. I bought a red backpack and typed a label that said, Tilly. On the black and white composition notebook, I made a cover that said The Adventures of Tilly...there are several volumes.

Tilly would also come out of his bag to sit on the couch in my classroom. If a student was displaying a behavior that was unacceptable, that student could sit on the couch and write why he or she was misbehaving. They could also write about something exciting that happened that day as well. Now imagine the line to write in the journal and talk to Tilly. Soooo, I had to just limit it to the weekend and leave the writing to the writing center.

Tilly had been to places I have never been to, like Niagara Falls. Each Monday, the student who had him for the weekend would read what Tilly's adventures were. All students gave their undivided attention. They also had to draw a picture or take a picture and place in the book. You should see the wonderful stories. Tilly is a hit in my class. NOTE TO SELF: The mascot you choose, be sure to buy more than one. By the end of the year, it will be dirty, scuffed up, it may get lost, or the dog eats it. I am grateful for a parent who took Tilly home cleaned and sewed up any parts that were torn or dirty.

At the writing center, there are colored pencils, colorful pens, crayons, writing paper, envelopes, and stamps. You name it, it is there!! My love for Office Depot and Staples certainly came in handy when buying supplies for this center. When you create your center, be sure that it has multiples of the same supply. Restock often and read what your students write about. The good thing about when a student has time at the writing center, I do not correct their spelling unless they ask me to. I want them to feel free to write and not worry about their spelling. I put several picture dictionaries there for their use as well. There also is a word journal with lots of words they may want to use. The word wall is also a source for spelling. The following item is a list of things that I use in my writing center.

- Dictionary
- Stapler/staples/scissors
- Markers
- Stencils
- Shopping list paper
- Composition notebook to write in
- Drawing paper
- Stationery paper
- Crayons
- Colored pencils
- Fancy colorful pens
- Envelopes
- Stencils
- Stamps
- Lined paper
- Blank paper
- Construction paper

Make your writing center a great place where the supplies are easy to access. Of course, you have gone over the rules of the writing center. They know how to take supplies out and where to put them when they are done. Let's bring back the love of writing. Starting with a Tilly and making the writing center inviting will help.

CHAPTER 7

October

Important Dates

OCTOBER 1 — *Fire Prevention Day*

OCTOBER 15 — *Hispanic Heritage Month ends*

OCTOBER 24 — *United Nation's Day*

OCTOBER 28 — *Statue of Liberty Day*

OCTOBER 31 — *Halloween*

Monthly Themes

National Pizza and Popcorn Month

Oktoberfest – *First Week*

Child Health Day – *First Monday*

Universal Children's Day – *First Monday*

Columbus Day – *Second Monday*

Thanksgiving Day in Canada – *Second Monday*

t's midway through October and we are finishing up the first quarter. The students are learning at a good rate. They know how to behave in class, they know the rules, they know where to find supplies in the room. They can identify short vowels, long vowels, and special sounds. They can recognize a mistake in a sentence and make the necessary corrections. We have to find a reason to celebrate and here is one way we do it.

Writing

Learning to write is an integral part of a student's life. This is the time they learn to put what is in their heads on paper. They begin at an early age wanting to hold crayons and pencils making circles or drawing pictures of partial people. I get excited around this time of the year because I know that in my class, my students will be getting ready to learn about the writing process. They will learn the steps to make a piece of work perfect by using the 5 steps of the writing process.

> I know that my students may not understand how to even begin editing a paper, but we work together.

I begin on the second week of school by giving the students a half sheet of paper called Write Rights. The students must find the mistakes, correct and edit the paper. I know that my students may not understand how to even begin editing a paper, but we work together. I love finding resources that are so useful to the classroom. Writing A-Z has played a gigantic part in helping my students to understand how to edit papers and look for grammatical errors. I use it for morning work. This half sheet of paper not only concentrates on editing, but it has the parts of speech, spelling, contractions, capitalization, punctuation, you name it, it is there. There are 30 weeks of these papers labeling each day of the week. If I ever forget to have one waiting on their desk in the morning, I'm in trouble. These papers also include a rule sheet for that specific skill they are learning about for the week. It explains to them how and why we use each rule. They are aligned with the Common Core State Standards, so I don't have to worry about if I should use them or not. The Write Rights goes up to 6th grade. This site offers a multitude of resources. Feel free to get a subscription, it is well worth the money.

October is when I introduce and implement the writing process. Since the beginning of the school year, I have instilled in my students my love for reading and they too have become avid lovers of books. We have learned how to properly care for books, where to read them in class, when to read them and how they can make our imagination come to life and take us to places we have never been. The books in our classroom library are differentiated, so each student knows the exact book they can pick up and read. My books are color-coded green, blue, yellow, and red. Each book has a specific color sticker to match the bin it belongs to. My students have been tested and know what levels they

> I have instilled in my students my love for reading and they too have become avid lovers of books.

I bought this chair from a Thrift Store for $8.
It was white, but I spray painted it a glossy black from Home Depot.
The words are painted on with 3-D bubble paint.

are on. The reading specialist tests each student at the beginning of the year and quarterly after that. I also use Accelerated Reading (AR) to test them weekly. They choose the appropriate book to read according to their color. I talk with my students about becoming actual authors and illustrators. We dissect books and learn all about each part.

Our class learns how to write different pieces such as an opinion piece, writing to inform, and using writing with illustrations. They learn and know what the parts of a story are...the beginning, middle, and end. They can write to inform. They know the difference between fiction and non-fiction. When they write, they are given a guideline to follow for the rough draft. Once they have completed their checklists, they can write their stories. Their stories are displayed, and they can sit in the author's chair to read their work to the class. That's a great way to celebrate. They have been waiting for their writing to be approved just to get the chance to sit in this coveted chair. The pride on their faces when they read is picture-worthy.

Community Dioramas

This month in Social Studies, we learn about our communities, cultures, and the world we live in. We explore different types of maps and try to figure out where we live on the map. With technology

today, we never have to be lost. We use this technology to find out where we are on a neighborhood map of our school. The students are excited that we can put in an address and the location and pictures pop up on the screen.

It is important that students are familiar with the communities they live in. Some communities can be rural, urban, or suburban. Most of the students in my class recognize that

they live in urban areas or the suburbs. They are able to identify their surroundings. They are excited about knowing their addresses and how to write them properly. Once they have mastered what a community is, they are now ready to celebrate by completing a community diorama of their specific communities.

The projects that come in are elaborate and very detailed. The students have to present their communities to the class. All projects are displayed in the foyer of the school for all to see. There are many different ways to make a diorama. Essentially, it is a shoebox. They make an outline of their different communities and create it inside of this shoebox. I remember when my son was in my class, I helped him make his. I used the templates of houses and buildings from the social studies book and glued them to a foam board. We put houses, a Target, a Chipotle, buildings, and all the things in our neighborhood. You can be creative and make all these things or you can go to a craft store and find all you need to make one.

The students were proud of their work and couldn't wait for everyone to see it in the foyer of the school after the Diorama Museum in the classroom. These are just the dioramas displayed on the student's

> **When you set the expectations high for your students, they really want to achieve them.**

desks... gotta make it sound fancy. When you set the expectations high for your students, they really want to achieve them. When I taught my son, and I was helping him to complete his project, he constantly reminded me of what I said in the classroom. He repeated how I said that it must be neat, must have a 3D element, and how he should be creative. He wanted his diorama to be neat and look good. I gave each of the students a rubric to follow and did you know, he held me to it. I was proud of him because I didn't know that he was listening to what I said in the classroom. Know that your students go home and repeat whatever you say in the classroom, good or bad. Set the standard high, they will follow through.

Apple Week

Do you like apples? I love apples! October is such a great month when apples are soooo good. Pink Lady, McIntosh, Delicious Red, Honey Crisp... my ultimate favorite... so many to choose from. I've never been apple picking but planning a field trip for my class to go apple picking is in the near future. Since we can't go apple picking, I'm bringing the apples to them. I had been teaching lessons on comparing and contrasting, things that are alike and different, and sharing your opinion in writing. I started the week off with a chart. I brought in 4 different types of apples: red, yellow, green, and honey crisp. That day, we read about apples and the surprise was a taste test of apples. I cut up the apples and put toothpicks in them. Each student tasted all four of the apples and had to choose the apple that they liked the best. I made tiny apples that they had to tape to the chart in the column of the apple that they liked best. After they finished, we made a graph of the apples. They also had to make up one or two math questions using the vocabulary, more, less, or fewer. So many different lessons to be taught. Using cross-curricular subjects is like killing two birds with one stone.

The next day, we made apple cider. We read a story about sitting around a campfire drinking warm apple cider. We found a great, simple recipe. We also included math in this lesson as well. The students had to help me measure the ingredients. I brought in different measuring devices and they had to help me choose the one that worked best. We pretended we were at a campfire and drank our apple cider, which turned out to be deeelicious!!

On Wednesday, we watched videos on how farmers harvest apples. They saw how to make apple cider and apple sauce. The students had to write an opinion piece on why they liked or disliked the apple cider or the apples. It was such a fun week.

Thursday, we made apple sauce!! (inserts screaming, jumping up and down, and doing the splits). I brought in green apples, gala, honey crisp, and red apples. I gave each student half of an apple, a plate, and a plastic knife. Each student had to cut up the apples into chunks. After the apples were cut up, we poured all apples into the crockpot. I then chose students to measure the ingredients to put into the crockpot. They stirred it up and then put the lid on it. It cooked for four hours on high. We did this early in the morning, so it would be done by the end of the day. My students couldn't focus, nor could the students that were walking by in the hallway. The smell was extremely delightful. Everyone peeked their heads in the class to find out what we were cooking. I let the students check the progress of the apples throughout the day.

The apples were getting softer, but not soft enough to mash with a stainless-steel masher. I was getting depressed because I wanted the students to taste the applesauce we were making that day. Then I remembered, that a parent sent in a hand-held emulsifier. I got it out, plugged it in, and voila! The apples began to turn into applesauce. I couldn't believe my eyes. I was so happy. WE MADE APPLESAUCE!!! The kids were jumping up and down just as I was. Everyone then tasted the warm applesauce we made. It was very good. We shared it with the teachers in the building and even the principal. My students went home and shared what they learned. I had parents texting and emailing for the recipe. One parent told me now her son won't eat store-bought applesauce anymore, she has to make it for him. That's good news!! Totally love it.

On the last day, we made apple pops. I brought in chocolate, white chocolate, and caramel that we melted so they could smother the apples in it. I also brought in pretzels that we crumbled up, M&M's, and sprinkles to decorate the apple pops. It was a messy day, but they had fun ending apple week. We let them sit until they were cool. I wrapped them in Saran Wrap and they took them home. What a day!

Teachers, you CAN be creative. You are a teacher because you love kids. You want the best for them. You want them to learn all they can and have fun doing it. Put on your thinking caps as I say to my students and think of all the amazing ways to make your class fun and engaging. Your students will love you for it. Now you may have to come out of pocket like I do, but it's worth the smiles in the end. Some parents may volunteer to send in items if you let them know ahead of time. But since I teach at a private school, I hate for them to spend money for anything extra.

> Now you may have to come out of pocket, like I do, but it's worth the smiles in the end.

Homemade Applesauce

- 10–12 apples
- ¾ cups of water
- 1 tsp cinnamon
- ½ cup sugar

1. Peel & dice apples
2. Put all ingredients in crockpot
3. Stir, cover 4–5 hours
4. Mash apples
5. Let cool and eat.

CHAPTER 8

November

Important Dates

NOVEMBER 1 — *Author's Day*

NOVEMBER 11 — *Veterans Day*

NOVEMBER 19 — *Discovery Day in Puerto Rico*

NOVEMBER 21 — *World Hello Day*

NOVEMBER 26 — *Sojourner Truth Day*

NOVEMBER 29 — *Louisa May Alcott's Birthday*

NOVEMBER 30 — *Mark Twain's Birthday*

Monthly Themes

Election Day *– Tuesday after the first Monday*

Thanksgiving Day *– Fourth Thursday*

November is here and it's time we learn about Native Americans, how communities were in the past. My students are able to compare and contrast things that happened long ago to now. It's so funny how I can show them pictures of an old rotatory phone, a telephone booth, or a phone book and they do not know what it is. This is the month we honor our Veterans who have fought hard for us. We write letters and thank them for their service. We learn all about Thanksgiving and why it is celebrated. We make crafts and prepare to have a wonderful Thanksgiving lunch at school. What is also special about this month is that we have been preparing the book that our class will have published. The students are excited about it and can't wait to see it.

Publish a Book/Authors Party/Illustrators

We are well into the second quarter of school. My first graders are legit writers and illustrators. They can read a story or book and write about it with a drawn picture. They can clearly give their opinions and state whether they like it or not, with evidence. I get them excited about a book that my previous classes wrote. They are thrilled because they didn't believe that 6 and 7-year old kids can write a book. Then I tell them that they will become authors and illustrators and that the book the class writes will be published, and people can really buy it.

After they have learned the five steps of the writing process: (Author House, Author Advice)

- *Prewriting.* You're ready to start writing
- *Writing.* OK, so now you have your plan, start writing
- *Revision.* Your story can change a great deal during this stage
- *Editing.* You have overhauled your story
- *Publishing.* Let's read your awesome work!

We begin to write the pages for our book. Each child receives two full pages of the book. One to write their story on with lines and the other to illustrate it.

There is a company called Student Treasures. This company publishes student-written books for free. They send you all of the materials you will need to help you get started on your classroom book. I have used this company for more than 6 years, and each year, they get better. They even give the teacher a copy of the book for free, with coupons to buy 3 at a discount. I will include their information in the resource chapter.

After each child has written their story of why they chose a certain career, we have a Career Day in our class. Each student comes dressed in the attire of the career they chose. I get parent volunteers to come in and speak to the students about their jobs. One time, I had a parent who was a dentist come in and do demonstrations for the kids on how to brush their teeth. She had goody bags of toothpaste, toothbrushes, and treats for the students. It was a fun day.

After the presentations, I had a photoshoot for the kids. All of these pictures would go in the class book. By the way, we named the book Small Kids, Big Dreams. There are several volumes to this book. Each year we add another volume to the collection.

The next part of the book is illustrating. Each student drew a picture for their second page to put in the book. They drew pictures of them doing their jobs. After all of the pictures were drawn, they color the picture with watercolor markers. The book comes together nicely. With the pictures that I took of each student, I arranged them to match their story and picture. It just takes a bit of organization to put it together. I always create an outline for how I want it to go. The publishing company also gives directions on how to put it together. Of course, I had to add my own touch to it.

Once the book is complete and all of the steps have been followed, I mail off the book. Parents have the opportunity to order these books. I usually get the books before Thanksgiving break. Most parents order 3–5 books to give away as Christmas gifts. The books start at $19.99, but who can put a price on a piece of work that your child has had published?

I have been pumping up the students and parents. Everyone is excited to see this book, a hardback book at that. We have an Author's party (book signing and reading). My students are actually authors and illustrators. I arrange a time during the day when the parents can come in and listen to their child read their story from the book. We even invite the principal. Parents volunteer to bring in food. It works out really well because we also use this celebration for our class Thanksgiving dinner. Everyone is dressed up. The books are displayed. I even make 8x10 black and white glossies, so the kids can sign them for their parents. It's a keepsake that the parents and students never get rid of.

BROOKE SCOTT
Police Officer

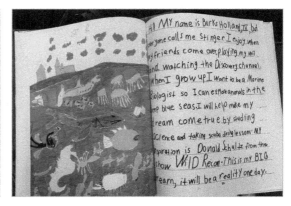

Hi! MY name is Burke Holland II but everyone calls me Stinger. I enjoy when my friends come over playing my wii and watching the Discovery chanael. when I grow up I want to be a Marine biologist so I can explore animals in the deep blue seas. I will help make my dream come true by studing science and taking scuba diving lessons. MY inpiration is Donald Schultz from the show WID Recon. This is my BIG dream, it will be a reality one day.

Always celebrate your student's accomplishments. It makes them proud and happy to know that they have done such a spectacular thing, such as becoming an author and an illustrator. The students keep these books forever and can look back at them and see their work from first grade. This book can now go in your class library for the next class to read.

Thanksgiving

As teachers, we have a lot to be grateful for. Just having a job to teach and enlighten students are blessings to me. As I sit back and think of all of the amazing students I have encountered during my teaching, I feel honored and truly thankful for the opportunity to educate them. It's a blessing when after years have gone by and you see a student and they tell you something they remembered you teaching them. They tell me how much I have influenced them to be a Superstar. Superstar meaning everything they do, they do it with all their might. Do it with a smile, do it with an open mind, and do it to put you on the right track to becoming successful. I call my students Superstars because they are. They are precious in my sight but most precious to God. They watch celebrities on TV and aspire to be like them, I tell them that it's not easy work to be on TV. There are certain milestones that one must cross to get there. Hard work is one of them. I tell them they can be superstars, superstars of their homework, of their careers, of anything that they put their minds to. I am thankful that I am able to instill the little wisdom that I have into them.

So in this month of November, we tell reasons why we are thankful each day. I love them to write in their journals. Each day, only if it is one word and a picture, I ask that they write what they are thankful for. Each student gets a day to read what they wrote in their journals. If it is private, they have the option of just telling one thing they are thankful for.

We start at the beginning of the month collecting canned goods and non-perishable items to bless someone with a basket from first grade. One year, there was a family at our school who had lost everything in a fire and was in need of food, clothes, and even simple toiletries, things we take for granted. Students also brought in turkeys. They were excited to know that they could help someone have a meal to eat. The food was coming in non-stop. That year, we gave the baskets to this family in our school. The funny thing about it is, they were bringing in items as well. They didn't know that we would give it to them. They were truly thankful. So, if you can and are allowed, start a little food bank or pantry to help someone who is in need. It is a lesson the students will never forget of how to help others. They're never too young to begin this lesson, they'll never forget it and make it a part of their daily lives. I know this for a fact. I told you I taught my son Stinger in first grade and we did this project. Every year from then on, he wanted to find a project to help others who were in need. To this day, we have not stopped.

We learn about the first Thanksgiving and why it was so important to the Native Americans. We are still comparing, and we talk about life back then and now. There's always a writing opportunity. I give to those who need, a sentence stem

> Be responsible for helping to make a difference, not only in November, but always.

and they can go from there. We celebrate Thanksgiving by having a nice meal with the entire school.

Find reasons to be thankful. Talk about the kids who have no food, clothes, or shelter right here in the United States. Be responsible for helping to make a difference, not only in November but always.

CHAPTER 9

December

Important Dates

DECEMBER 6 — *Sinterklaas Day in the Netherlands*

DECEMBER 7 — *Pearl Harbor Day*

DECEMBER 10 — *Human Rights Day*

DECEMBER 13 — *Santa Lucia's Day in Sweden*

DECEMBER 15 — *Bill of Rights Day*

DECEMBER 25 — *Christmas*

DECEMBER 26 — *First day of Kwanzaa*

DECEMBER 26 — *Boxing Day in Canada and England*

DECEMBER 31 — *New Year's Eve*

Monthly Themes

Hanukkah *– 25th day of the Jewish month of Kislev*

Personal Narrative

My first graders have done a wonderful job learning to write different types of papers. We are now to the point when they are beginning to write personal narratives. When I introduce a new concept to my students, I always make it entertaining. You are on your classroom stage. They love hearing stories about my life...and I like telling them...LOL!!! It makes for a better lesson and when they recall information about a topic, they seem to remember it more.

So, now it's time to write about personal narratives? They ask, Mrs. Holland, what is that? I explain spinning around, ohhhh, I'm sooo glad you asked. That's a fabulous question in my best Blair from Facts of Life sitcom voice...hehehehe! Now I have their attention. I have all hands and eyes on me. I ask them if they have ever heard of a narrator. They say, yes, it's a person who tells the story. OMG! I high -five that person because they are soooo right! Geniusssss!

> When I introduce a new concept to my students, I always make it entertaining.

Then I begin to tell them what personal is. I ask, can Jordan tell the story that is in Hazel's head? They say, no. I said, can Zane tell a story that is in Sean's head? They say, nope because whatever is in Sean's head, Zane doesn't know. I said, absolutely correct. So, a personal narrative is something that is only personal to you, no one else knows about it. You are the person telling the story, so you are the narrator. They say, ohhhhh! Thumbs up, we totally get that. Then I say, can either of you tell my personal narrative, they say of course not. Only you know what's inside your head, not us. I say you got that right, with a big thumbs up. Then I whisper, who wants to tell a personal narrative about the principal? They say, huh? I say it again, then they say, we can't tell his personal narrative, we're not him. Then I say, well I'll tell you one about me. Hmmmm, what shall I tell you about? By now, they are yelling, tell me about your sisters, tell me about Stinger, tell me about your husband. I say, who said that? And a shy hand goes up and I say, welllll, you read my mind, I'll tell you about my wedding day. They screamed yayyyyy! I began really soft to get their attention.

The objective is, to get students to write a personal narrative with events in chronological order. They also must draw pictures to represent their story. So I put my title on the board: My Wedding Day. I start off by drawing my hands and feet because the first thing I did that morning was get my fingernails and toes manicured. They immediately said, but you had to wake up first and eat breakfast. I said you're right. But I don't want to include that because the reader can infer that. So, I continue to draw pictures, me going to pick daisy flowers for our bouquets, getting my make-up done, taking pictures all the way until I kissed the groom...they giggled and said ewww... LOL!!!

I then go back over my story and mix it all up. I start by eating at the reception, then waking up, and then kissing the groom. I then say, do you understand my story, and they said no because you did not go in chronological order. See how they are using the vocabulary from the content provided. So they totally get the point. So, I say stand up if you're ready to write your personal narrative. They all jump up. One student says, what shall we write about, we didn't get married. I said, weeelllll, your story is going to be about your best memory in first grade. You can choose anything that you remember in first grade...good or bad. Now, who's ready to begin? I give each student a graphic organizer to jot their ideas down and they get started on their personal narratives.

The moral of the story, whatever you are teaching, make it personal to the students or something that they can

> Whatever you are teaching, make it personal to the students or something that they can relate too.

relate to. When students think they know you and you know them, they are more willing to perform at a higher standard to please you. They will be eager to show you what their rough draft looks like. Some couldn't decide what was their "bestest" memory because they had so many. I read one little girl's title, The Day I Met Mrs. Holland, she had begun to write her story and wanted my approval on what she had written so far. I read it and if you know me, I got all teary-eyed. Be real with your students and they'll be really great with you.

The month of December is also exciting for students because they know that Christmas is coming soon. And who doesn't love Christmas? In social studies, we learn about traditions around the world. They learn about how other children celebrate different holidays and Christmas is one of them. I have found books in our library or YouTube videos to show the students how holidays are celebrated. My students are then grouped together to discuss and come up with a written report on the holiday they were given. They work together, also at home to prepare for their presentations. The reports are on a poster board with pictures and a short report on the given holiday.

The excitement about Christmas begins with me. I love to decorate my class for Christmas. I use my reading tree and a Christmas tree. I hang lights, garland, and whatever craft we worked on in class on the tree. I hang Christmas bulbs from the ceiling. I have small decorated trees around the room. The best part of it all is deciding what to decorate our classroom door with. As a class, we discuss what we think will be best. Each year, our class has won the Christmas door decorating contest. One year, we read about penguins and I saw a wonderful penguin door that a friend of mine created for her classroom door. I went to another favorite site, Pinterest, to see how others were making penguins and I then came up with my own version. I used all of the resources I had in my classroom and the school resource room. I really didn't want to spend a lot of money on this door. I stayed after school to complete it with the help of a

few students who didn't want to wait until the next day to see it. I freehand drew out all the parts to the penguin....I am so not an artist...hehehehehe. I miss the art teacher, Mrs. Watson, at Dupont; she was my savior for all things that needed to be drawn. I knew that I wanted a huge penguin on the door, but I have two doors, so I had to come up with something for the other door. I love to see penguins sliding down the snow, so, there was my idea. I'd make small penguins but put the faces of my students on them with cute little hats. They would be sliding down the snow on the door. Soooo, cute!

I know that you have those creative juices flowing in you. Sometimes, it's hard to get them going. Some teachers are put in a box and told exactly what to do, but you can remedy that. Do what they ask but put a twist on it. There are a million ways to teach 1+1. You just have to be bold enough to put your thang on it. Now, if you have just taken this teaching job because it was the easiest thing to do, you'll have a problem. I can't sleep at night because I have so many ideas that I can't wait to use in the classroom. I want my students to be lifelong learners. I want them to have fun learning. I want them to have prior experiences that will spark their imagination to want to learn. It's so important that you are excited about what you do each day. If you are a boring teacher, your students take on your personality. Be hype, be loud, sing, dance, enjoy it and they will, too. Excited teachers ignite the minds of their students.

> Excited teachers ignite the minds of their students.

CHAPTER 10

January

Important Dates

JANUARY 6   *New Year's Day*

JANUARY 2   *Good Luck Day*

JANUARY 5   *George Washington Carver's Birthday*

JANUARY 11   *Banana Split Day*

JANUARY 11   *Mrs. Holland's Birthday*

JANUARY 16   *Religious Freedom Day*

JANUARY 20   *Presidential Inauguration Day*

JANUARY 22   *Eleven Cities Race in the Netherlands*

JANUARY 23   *National Handwriting Day*

Monthly Themes

Chinese New Year
First day of the new moon using the Chinese calendar

Martin Luther King Jr's Day – *Third Monday*

School Nurse Day – *Fourth Wednesday*

appy New Year!! We are back from the Christmas vacation and are ready to hop back into the swing of things. I know you are wondering if I gave my students a "Christmas packet". Nope, I sure didn't...LOL! I truly believe that students should read every day, but when on vacation, I believe in a brain break. This doesn't mean that all learning ceases, it means that I am truly giving them a minute from doing things that "seem" like it is school-related. I want them to enjoy their break and not task parents with overseeing busy work because I was being selfish. I simply gave my students a Winter Challenge to complete. OK, you're saying, that's "busy work", Mrs. Holland...LOL, but it really isn't. One of my favorite go-to websites when I am looking for anything is Teachers Pay Teachers. Type what you are looking for or have a general idea of what you want....and voila...it pops up. Of course, these resources come with a price, but it is well worth it. Anywhooo, The Brown Bag Teacher is one of the stores I frequent on TpT. She is a teacher currently teaching a combo K/1 class in Kentucky. I totally love her energy and love for teaching. Her store has tons of resources for K-1st grade teachers. She creates great resources for teachers who know what they are looking for, but don't have the means to create it themselves, like me! You should check her out.

Now back to this challenge. It is a two-week challenge that spans over the days given for Christmas break. The activities on the calendar include read in your PJs, read aloud in a silly voice, or read a recipe and read with your sunglasses on. All of the activities are fun. I don't want to give them all, but you get the gist of it. Not "schoolwork". Parents can put the calendar on the fridge and each day students mark off that they have completed the activity. If your students are traveling during the break, they can take it with them. Of course, I made this sound so exciting. I didn't make it mandatory, but I did offer a reward for those students who completed it. See, not so bad, right?

After teaching for a long period of time, I look forward to these breaks. They come on time and are much needed. By Christmas, I am certainly ready to refresh my mind and take a brain break. But you are reading about a true, passionate teacher who never stops working. I am always finding new ways to implement a concept, I am always online finding what lesson I can buy to create a rigorous lesson or writing lesson plans so I don't have to spend my Sunday preparing for class. Although your educational ethics may not be like mine, I hope that you are in this for all the right reasons. You are a teacher because you love kids, you want them to be successful, you want to make them lifelong learners and become leaders, you want to change their lives. These are the attributes that I wish to leave behind. I cannot stress it enough.

My Birthday

Every year on my birthday, I throw a birthday party for my class. Everyone gets balloons, party hats, cupcakes, and a goody bag. I make my favorite food, haystacks for lunch which is basically a taco salad with the works. I read my favorite book. I have so many,

but that day I show them a few and they get to choose which one I will read. After the story is read, they then have to write the beginning, middle, and end to the story. I have so many wonderful graphic organizers for them to choose from that I have collected over the years. A great math lesson...I give them my age and they have to try and figure out what year I was born in or give them the year I was born in and they figure out my age. That's a great reason to celebrate. There is still teaching and learning (which my principal says MUST happen... LOL) although we are celebrating my birthday.

Dr. Martin Luther King, Jr. was born in January. Another reason to celebrate. We begin the study of his life. We learn how he helped to improve our world and how he was a great leader. We watch videos and read books about him. I have made a bulletin board with quotes from him that will be discussed throughout the lessons. The students tell me what they know about him and we go from there. There are so many different resources with awesome lessons on MLK. I always go to my favorite site TpT to see what I can find on this great man. Another one of my favorite stores on that site is Education with an Apron. She has tons of social studies, history, and geography lessons that you can use with little to no prep. You can buy them in the monthly bundles. Her resources go up to 3rd grade. You will not regret the wonderful lessons she has...especially when it comes to teaching Black History. I had the privilege of meeting her at a wonderful conference called Get Your Teach On. Check her out.

A great lesson to be created about MLK is the timeline of his life. This is also the time I teach my students about another genre called biography. These two lessons can last the entire month and can lead us straight into Black History Month. I begin talking with my students about how they can show courage or if there ever was a time in their lives that they showed courage. Maybe they stood up for a friend on the playground, or even telling a boy or girl that you like him/her.

> Remember that you are always in the first 5 minutes of your lesson trying to get their attention and access prior knowledge.

Remember that you are always in the first 5 minutes of your lesson trying to get their attention and access prior knowledge. Now their juices are flowing, and you are able to get your point across. By now your students should know about chronological order. We talk about their routines in the morning. Do you eat first, then wake up, or do you wake up, brush your teeth, get dressed, etc. Do we discuss that? We then discuss the order of their lives. Were you born walking and talking? Did you eat a slice of pizza right away? So, they get the gist of chronological order.

After studying MLK's life, we are now able to actually make a timeline of events of his life. My students know how to take notes, they can stop and jot. They know that when they see dates, it must be important, so they always write dates down. I draw a timeline on the board. We start early in MLK's life. They know that only important items go on a timeline. They know that if MLK went to McDonald's to eat a burger, they should not add it to the timeline. They know that if

he graduated from high school at 15 in 1944 and went to Morehouse, it should be included on the timeline.

We have fun doing this. Each student is paired together with books to find important dates. After his timeline of events is complete, their project is to make a timeline of their lives. They know what to do and can go home and tell their parents exactly what is expected of them. A rubric is given as a guideline. Their projects are amazing. Seeing them as little babies and watching them grow on their timelines is priceless. I had one student present his timeline, well they all do, but he told me how he had a hole in his heart and had to have surgery. He had the pictures on his timeline. I asked him, why he chose to add those pictures? He said, he wanted everyone to know because it was an important event in his life, and now he was healthy. What a tearjerker. So, you see how if you are specific in your delivery of what you expect, projects will come back exceeding your expectations. We celebrate by displaying our timelines in the hallway for all to see. We also make a chronological order banner of the birthdays in our class. Of course, I'm the first one on the classroom birthday timeline.

The other lesson for this month is on how to write a biography. Students already have an idea of what it is. They interview each other and come up with specifics of their partner's life and write about it. I know you are saying, ok these are first graders, yep they are but they are very intelligent and can get the job done with guidance and a graphic organizer. We do this in class. There should be 5–6 sentences with a drawn picture. These turn out amazing.

CHAPTER 11

February

Important Dates

FEBRUARY 1 *National Freedom Day*

FEBRUARY 2 *Ground Hog Day*

FEBRUARY 8 *Boy Scout Day*

FEBRUARY 11 *Thomas Edison's Birthday*

FEBRUARY 12 *Abraham Lincoln's Birthday*

FEBRUARY 14 *Valentine's Day*

FEBRUARY 15 *Susan B. Anthony's Birthday*

FEBRUARY 22 *George Washington's Birthday*

FEBRUARY 29 *Leap Year Day*

Monthly Themes

Black History Month

National Heart Month

Dental Health Month

President's Day *– Third Monday*

Winter Olympic Games

February is one of my favorite months of the year. There are so many reasons to celebrate and we take full advantage of it in my class. We celebrate Valentine's Day, President's Day, but the entire month is Black History month and each day we learn about a different black historian who invented something, did something courageous or paved the way for blacks. I hope you can implement the activities and lessons we learn during this month in your class.

Black History Month

Our history and heritage are so important to us. Our ancestors have done so much for us to get us to where we are today. We celebrate them always, but the month of February is dedicated to our Black Historians who have paved the way for us with their talents and or courage. So, during this month, our class gets to know all of the Black Historians who they may not hear about on a regular basis.

Every morning, I introduce my students to a black historian. I write their name on the board. I then read all about that person. I try to find people who they haven't heard of. The lesson comes in when I have the students state specific facts about what they heard. I write them on the board. Each child has a pack of stickies at their desk. They have to copy from the board onto the sticky the name of the historian and the facts given. Each day they do this. Each sticky goes into their journal. By the end of the month, each student should have 20 stickies. Those students who have 20 at the end of the month will get to choose a reward out of the treasure box. My students love this activity and look forward to it each day. They absolutely love it!

Along with learning about a Black Historian each day, my students must write a report each week on a person of their choice who has made a difference in the world. I give them a list of about 36 people, they can use these or find them on their own. They usually surprise me and find ones that I have never heard of before, which is awesome. I give them the guidelines two weeks before the project begins. So in January, parents are notified of the expectations for these reports for February. They must follow these guidelines to a T. There is also a rubric attached with how many points they receive for each item, adding up to 50.

Every Thursday in the month of February, which equals 4 Thursdays, a report is due. They must be able to present the report to the entire class. I am sure to tell the students that they must do the work themselves. They must be able to tell me in their own words about this person. They also have to write it. They do such fabulous work. Every year, I'll have at least one parent who waits until the last minute and writes it out for their child. When that child comes to school to present, he/she is sad. They say, "I told my mom that I had to write it". They lose points, but next week, they get full credit because they followed the rubric and their child actually wrote it. You'll get those parents who will test you. Be firm, stick to your guns, and they will follow suit.

Each week, I create a bulletin board out of their reports for the entire school to see. They are proud to see their work on display. The other students in the school can read their work. I have pictures of some of the ones they have chosen, so I display those pictures with their reports.

I am extremely proud to tell my students that I had the pleasure of meeting someone who made history a long time ago. In my travels across the country, I have met some very influential and famous people. Sometimes I'm star struck and other times I'm ok, just happy to meet them. But one time, I was in awe. I give my students clues as to who it could have been and as soon as I gave them the last clue: She did not give up her seat on the bus...they immediately knew who it was, Rosa Parks. YES!! Screaming...I met Rosa Parks!!

My group Virtue sang at the famous Apollo Theater in New York City. There, different celebrity artists paid tribute to her in song. She sat there on the front row and enjoyed each act. After the show was over, we met her and took a picture. I was teary eyed because I knew what she had done for African Americans during the Civil Rights Movement. I gave her a hug. She was so little and fragile, yet strong. I told her thank you for not giving up her seat on that bus in Montgomery, Alabama. She shook her head with a smile and said I loved your song...screams inside!! I then show my students the picture and play the video of the Tribute to Rosa Parks Something Inside So Strong from YouTube. Meeting her was a day I will never forget.

That's me, standing on the right side of her.

To end the month, we celebrate Black History month with the first black person to ever become a living trademark. Her name is Nancy Green AKA Aunt Jemima. She was a slave, but she was a great cook, storyteller, and her personality was exceptional. When a company called Pearl Milling decided to develop and package a self-rising pancake mix, they needed someone to represent the brand. They found Nancy in Kentucky at age 56. She signed a lifelong contract to represent the brand. She traveled around the world and made this company a lot of money.

I bring in my griddle, the pancake mix, syrup, whip cream, and fruit toppings and we eat pancakes all day. Thank you, Aunt Jemima, for being the first living trademark. Nancy was the spokesman for the company until she died in a car crash in 1923.

What a way to end black history month! Celebrate! Always find a reason to celebrate.

February is such an eventful busy month. I have to pick and choose what to celebrate or I'll be broke. But I can't forget about Valentine's Day. We learn all about love...your students will say, "Ewwww" and giggle. We learn why this day is celebrated. I ask each student to bring in a small shoebox. We decorate it with stickers and whatever

else we have on hand in the class that's related to Valentine's. We also make a little Valentine puppet from a red cup. I found this on Pinterest, but there are so many other activities that you can make for this special day. I give the parents a list of all the students in the class. They make Valentine's cards or buy them already made with candy attached. I know this is a day of sweets, but then they go home... LOL! Secretly, I love when they bring me Valentine's... they're always so cute. I hoard them. I know I should purge, but I hate getting rid of special gifts students give to me. Again, you want to make lasting memories and I have them forever.

CHAPTER 12

March

Important Dates

MARCH **6** — *Doll's Festival Day in Japan*

MARCH **8** — *International Women's Day*

MARCH **10** — *Harriet Tubman Day*

MARCH **12** — *Girl Scout Founder's Day*

MARCH **15** — *Ides of March*

MARCH **17** — *St. Patrick's Day*

MARCH **21** — *Children's Poetry Day*

Monthly Themes

National Nutrition Month

National Reading Month

Red Across America Day

National Crafts Month

Music in Our Schools Month

Reading

Speaking of reading, let's take another quick detour.

Reading time can be difficult. When I was in school, we read aloud, round-robin style or popcorn reading. I was comfortable doing this, but I noticed that there were students who were nervous about reading out loud. Today, there are so many different ways to teach reading without making a student feel self-conscious about not knowing how to sound out a word. Some students are shy and may not be ready to take on reading in front of the class. Research has proven that this type of reading often paralyzes the child. They tune out the other person who is reading, they are distracted, or read ahead. Some students even get in trouble while waiting on the other person to read. Todd Finley from the article 11 Alternatives for "Round Robin" and "Popcorn" Reading gives three good reasons not to use this type of reading.

1. STIGMATIZES POOR READERS. Imagine the terror that English-language learners and struggling readers face when made to read in front of an entire class.
2. WEAKENS COMPREHENSION. Listening to a peer orally read too slowly, too fast, or too haltingly weakens the learners' comprehension.
3. SABOTAGES FLUENCY AND PRONUNCIATION. Struggling readers model poor fluency skills and pronunciation. When instructors correct errors, fluency is further compromised.

Finley also found 11 different ways to better approach round-robin reading and here are a few ways:

1. CHORAL READING
2. SILENT READING
3. PARTNER READING
4. PALS (PEER-ASSISTED LEARNING STRATEGIES
   (PALS) pair strong and weak readers who take turns reading, re-reading, and retelling.

5. TEACHER ALOUD READING

   This activity, says Julie Adams of Adams Educational Consulting, is perhaps one of the most effective methods for improving student fluency and comprehension, as the teacher is the expert in reading the text and models how a skilled reader reads using appropriate pacing and prosody (inflection). Playing an audiobook achieves similar results.

6. ECHO READING

7. SHARED READING/MODELING

   By reading aloud while students follow along in their own books, the instructor models fluency, pausing occasionally to demonstrate comprehension strategies.

8. THE CRAZY PROFESSOR READING GAME

   To bring the text to life, students:

   - Read orally with hysterical enthusiasm.
   - Reread with dramatic hand gestures.
   - Partner up with a super-stoked question asker and answerer.
   - Play "crazy professor" and "eager student" in a hyped-up overview of the text.

9. BUDDY READINGS

   Kids practice orally reading a text in preparation for reading to an assigned buddy in an earlier grade.

10. TIME REPEATED READINGS

    This activity can aid fluency, according to literacy professors Katherine Hilden and Jennifer Jones. After an instructor reads (with expression) a short text selection appropriate to the students' reading level (90-95 percent accuracy), learners read the passage silently, then again loudly, quickly, and dynamically. Another kid graphs the times and errors so that children can track their growth.

11. FORI

    With Fluency-Oriented Reading Instruction (FORI), primary students read the same section of a text many times over the course of a week. Here are the steps:

- The teacher reads aloud while students follow along in their books.
- Students echo read.
- Students choral read.
- Students partner read.
- The text is taken home if more practice is required, and extension activities can be integrated during the week.

One way I read with students is in small groups. This way, the students feel comfortable reading for me. When students come to guided reading, each child has a book and they read to themselves. They are reading loud enough for me to hear, but not disturbing the others in the group. I walk around the table to hear each one read. This is a no-pressure type of reading as well. After we discuss the book, we pull out vocabulary words, nouns, verbs, and elaborate on the order of the book, so many lessons to gather from. By the time we are finished with the book, everyone has read the book several times. They absolutely love being called to their groups to read.

    I decide who is in the different groups by having each student tested by the reading specialist. She does running records and is able to tell me what level they are on. This method of assessing reading is done quickly and frequently. It is an individually conducted formative assessment that is ongoing and curriculum-based. I also use another form of testing through Accelerated Reading as mentioned before. Each child takes a test on the computer by answering comprehension questions and vocabulary to the best of their knowledge. These questions are based on the student who is taking the test. If the questions are too simple and the student is flying through the test, it gives them more challenging questions until they can't go any further. This program AR informs me of where they excelled and where they need help. It will also group the students according to their abilities and levels.

After the results are in, I announce to the students who's in what group. They get together and make up a name for their group. At times when it is difficult for them to decide, I will suggest using football teams, types of animals, colors, etc. Of course, I have pumped them up about these names, so they are excited. I use a guided reading chart to help me during my allotted reading time.

While students are meeting with me at the guided reading table, the others go to the chart to find out what they are to do until I call their groups. This can only run seamlessly if you have practiced, rehearsed, and practice again until your students can do this by themselves without disturbing other groups. If your students have not been taught what to do, they WILL be loud, disturb you, not do what they were assigned, and get into all types of other things.

If you look at the picture of me with the guided reading group, you will see a light on. My students know not to disturb me when I am in a group if this light is on. I have seen other teachers wear big

hats, silly big glasses, and put up signs when in reading groups. They may ask another student or try to figure it out for themselves. This maximizes all of the precious reading time. I have prepared each of the centers ahead of time, so students can get to work right away. After 15 or 20 minutes, the timer goes off and they switch. The key is preparation. Do it ahead of time, so you can focus on your group. I got this chart at Lakeshore Learning. It's called a Literacy Center Management chart.

During the month of March, we read a different book each day. I challenge the students to read at least 50 or more books for the month. This seems like a lot, but it's a challenge for them and they actually read more than the given amount. At the end of the month, the students have to choose their favorite book from the books they have read. I get them excited about what they are going to do at the end of the previous month. I tell them that now they get to become their favorite character. I tell them they will have a project to complete. This project is called the Brown Bag Book Report. Each student must choose a favorite character from the book, dress like that character, and choose 5 items from the book that is significant in the story to put into the brown bag (doesn't have to be a brown bag) and present it to the class. Oh my, oh my!! They go all out with this project. I have given them a rubric weeks before, so no one has an excuse for not knowing what to do. The key is keeping your parents informed. You have to make it sound exciting for them as well.

My classroom library has lots of books on different levels that are labeled. My students have access to these books all day long. When they finish their work, I can usually find them sitting under my tree reading, on the carpet, or the bean bag. My students not only read these books but, after they are finished reading, they can test their comprehension on Accelerated Reading. This online testing system has thousands of books to test students for comprehension and reading ability. I try to make sure that all of the books in my library are AR testable. They take an assessment to make sure they are

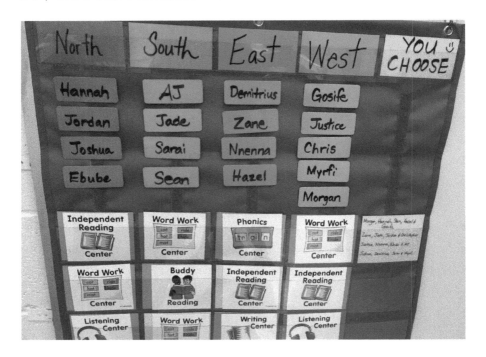

comprehending what they are reading. Each student has a reading goal. The goal is given after they have taken the initial tests. When the students reach their AR goal, there is definitely a celebration. They not only are celebrated in the classroom but in front of the entire school, quarterly.

Splash On Literacy

Have you ever wanted to read a book and create an art activity to go along with it? So many books make you want to be creative, but you just can't find the time to do so. I was on Instagram one evening and came across a post where kids were drawing after they had read a book. This page explained that Literacy and Art go hand in hand, I agreed. So, I investigated this site and fell in love with it. It is called Splash on Literacy. This

> **The key is keeping your parents informed. You have to make it sound exciting for them as well.**

company is out of Georgia and it has a studio where kids come in and are read a story, then they get to create a piece of art to accompany the reading. Every month, this company will send you a book and lesson plan. It will also come with all of the art supplies you will need for up to 30 students. I found this program to be a great help and resource to my class. They love to read and do art as well. This is one of my Fun Friday activities. They also send a sample of what the art should look like just in case you need it. Of course, this is for a monthly fee, but it is worth it. Check them out!

Here's one of the many activities we completed with Splash on Literacy.

Source: **A Bad Case of Stripes,** by David Shannon

CHAPTER 13

April

Important Dates

APRIL 1 — *April Fool's Day*

APRIL 7 — *World Health Day*

APRIL 18 — *Paul Revere's Ride*

APRIL 19 — *Patriot's Day*

APRIL 22 — *Earth Day*

Monthly Themes

Easter *(may fall in March)*

Passover
Begins on the 15th day of the Jewish month of Nisan

National Arbor Day *– Last Friday*

Take Your Daughter to Work Day *– Last Thursday*

National Poetry Month

Math Awareness Month

Library Week

April is National Poetry Month. Our class gets to express how they feel through poetry. We have learned about nouns, verbs, adjectives, and adverbs. They know how to rhyme and know how to correctly write a sentence. It's time to put what they know into action. Each day, I read a poem found in any children's poem book. Once a week, we actually write a poem. Here are some that we do: acrostic poem, adverb poem, alliteration poems, and similes.

In an Acrostic Poem, a word or person's name is written vertically down the left side of a page. These letters are used to begin each line of the poem. The acrostic, which usually does not rhyme, is written to characterize or describe the chosen word or person. This makes my students excited because we have mastered the concept of adjectives. I give each student a half piece of card stock, with their names down the left side. They then choose adjectives to represent each letter. After they are finished adding their adjectives, they decorate their cardstock. Then they choose several pieces of construction paper and use different craft scissors to make frames. They glue them all together to make a nice picture. They are then displayed.

The Adverb Poem was found on Super Teacher Worksheets, another favorite site I use. Students are to fill out the worksheet using adverbs to describe an action verb usually ending in -ly. After they chose their adverbs, they have to transfer them to a colorful sheet of paper I gave to them. They are to cut it out and glue it to a colored piece of cardboard stock. They also have to be creative and decorate it to match some of the words. They turn out amazing.

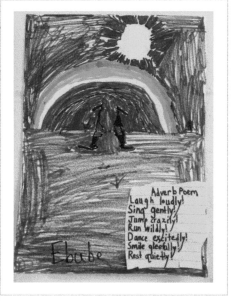

Of course with all the work you do with your students, find a way

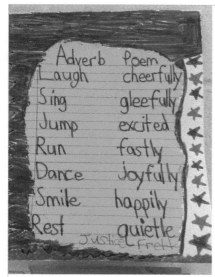

to display it so everyone can see. My bulletin boards and walls are covered with students Proud Work. Most will want to take it home but keep it for about a week, then send them home. When students see their work displayed, it makes them take ownership of their work. They will give their best each time because they know everyone will see it.

Alliteration Poem is several words that begin with the same letter or sound. This can be very fun for kids. This one is also a part of the CCSS. So, it aligns right along with what they are expected to learn.

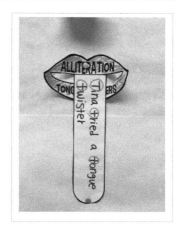

Similes are when two things are compared using "or" or "as", such as: as stubborn as a mule or slow as a turtle.

Tea Party/Egg Hunt

One of my favorite times of the year is Easter. OK! I know I have soooo many favorites...because I do. Whatever month Easter falls in March or April, but mostly in April, we have a grand tea party and Easter egg hunt. I try my hardest to turn this into a lesson, so we learn about the "Tea Party" and why it exists, which has nothing to do with our tea party, LOL So, if you were wondering, there is a little teaching and learning when I present this in class.

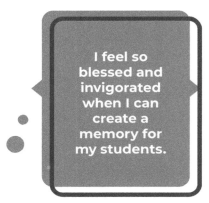

I feel so blessed and invigorated when I can create a memory for my students.

The tea party and egg hunt are special to me. I get the students excited because I tell them they have to dress in their fanciest clothes. That means wear your "bestest" outfit. Girls will wear frilly dresses with hats and gloves. Boys will come dressed in sharp suits, with bow ties, and hats looking handsome. Oh my! The excitement has already begun. I do this well over 2 to 3 weeks before the event, so parents have time to get their child's outfit together.

During the time before the event, we are watching etiquette videos on how to properly hold a teacup, manners, how to eat cucumber sandwiches, and so much more. See those are all mini-lessons...☺ Each boy gets to practice pulling out the chairs for the girls. All students are saying please and thank you, and they are practicing how not to put their elbows on the table... another lesson.

The anticipation comes in when I tell them about the invitation. I hand make the invitations and tell the students that only those students who have demonstrated their best behaviors will attend. So, for 2-3 weeks, students are being extra careful to follow all of the rules to get this coveted invite. I tell them that no one can enter the door of the tea party without the invitation. So, if you lose it, you can't come in. Now let me tell you something. All of the excuses parents make for their children when they lose something is ridiculous. When I tell you not one student lost that invitation or even wrinkled it. You must hold your students accountable. Make them responsible for their own actions. Teach them how not to make excuses. Excuses will get you nowhere in life. When students really want something, they truly know how to keep it safe, follow rules, and exemplify great behavior. So, baby, it's possible!

The same week that I give out the invitations. I don't give them all out on the same day. I make sure to give the first invitations to those students who have shown that they are Superstar Students. I have all week to give these out. The student who gets the first invitation is always extremely happy. This student has been on Great Day or above. The picture is the chart I use to keep track of behavior in my class and I really like it. I used to use the How Am I Doing chart from Lakeshore Learning with only 4 colors. I found that with that chart, the colors only went down Green=Great Behavior; Yellow=Check yourself; Orange=Consequence; Red=Contact parent. It never gave the student a chance to redeem himself or those students who displayed great behavior a chance to go even higher from there. So, I found this one on Really Good Stuff. I like the fact that there is always a chance for improvement in behavior. I said all of that to say, soooo if there are students who have not displayed great behavior, they are sure to get it together... LOL!

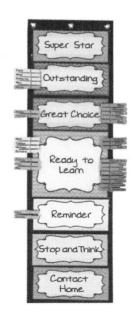

We dye eggs in the class the day before the tea party. I ask parents to send in a half dozen of hard-boiled eggs. I also ask them to send in Easter candy, an egg dying kit, and plastic eggs. Each group is assigned one of these to bring in. They bring in the materials and with the help of some parents, we dye the eggs in

> You must hold your students accountable. Make them responsible for their own actions. Teach them how not to make excuses.

class and stuff the plastic ones with candy or other treats. The next day, I ask older students to go outside to hide all of the eggs. This is the day of the tea party. There are two special eggs...a golden one for the big prize of a chocolate bunny and a silver egg for a smaller chocolate bunny.

The day before the party after school, it's time to decorate. I have bought all of the decorations for the room. I get help from select parents and we create such a beautiful setting for the kids. One year, I wanted to turn my room into a garden to have a Garden Tea Party and we certainly accomplished that. That year, I had my friends Mytonia Newman, Janice Vanderhorst, and Lawren Dolland help me. We stayed late that day. I borrowed flowers from the church across the way. Mrs. Rubin, the church secretary was so kind to let me come to the storage room and rummage through it until I found what I needed. The room was gorgeous with flowers and tulle hanging from the ceiling. The table settings had real porcelain china teacups and saucers, thanks to Mrs. Ocheing (a teacher at the school). When the kids walked in, there were so many ooohhh's and ahhhh's. The parents came in to take pictures and were so surprised.

Each year, the theme is different. All of the teachers come to take a peek and we even invite the principal to sip tea with us. The student's only request from him is that he must hold his pinky finger up when sipping his tea...LOL! Take a look at the pictures. When I tell you these students go all out, they come dressed to the 9's. They look so adorable. Of course, I am standing at the door dressed to the 9's, too. I have my hat and gloves and a frilly dress, too. They have their invitations in hand waiting to get in the door.

Once inside the room, we begin right away with tea and crumpets. They each get to choose the flavor of their tea. Sugar cubes and tiny spoons are on the table for their use. They are following their manners and using their inside voices. There are all sorts of other goodies on the serving table. The students are polite and patiently wait to choose their cucumber sandwiches, pimento cheese sandwiches, and egg salad sandwiches. Everyone has a stuffed belly in the end.

Then it's time to get the Easter baskets out and head outside for the egg hunt. The eggs have already been hidden outside on the playground. They are scanning the playground to see if they can spot that golden egg. I tell them the rules and then they are off yelling and screaming with excitement. The joy in their voices makes my heart smile. They are filling up their baskets with goodies. Then I hear a yelp, I found the golden egg! I run to check, but it's a yellow egg. Nope, that's not it. Another student says, is this the golden egg? I say, nope, that's still a yellow egg. Then four students come running, yelling Denilson found the golden egg. He has it in his hand. I say YES! That's theeee golden egg. They then run back out to find the silver egg. Oh, the joy!

I feel so blessed and invigorated when I can create a memory for my students. I always want to make lasting memories for them to look back on, don't you? (Inserts tears...LOL.) Teachers spend so much of their own money and a lot of extra time to make sure their classes are the best they can be. When my students actually remember not to put their elbows on the table, when the boys pull out the chairs for the girls, when they are using their manners throughout the party, it shows me that they were listening. Your students are listening to every word you say. Make those words count.

Teachers, you have these kids for more hours during the day than their parents. Do kind things for your students. It doesn't always

> **The joy in their voices makes my heart smile.**

take money. The lessons we teach them are valuable ones. They come to you with a blank slate. Put positive messages that they can be anything they want to be on that slate. Tell them hard work, perseverance, and staying focused is the key. These things will forever be etched in their minds as they choose the paths to become doctors, lawyers, teachers,

janitors, or firefighters. You can say, I had a part in helping a child to become successful. Now pat yourself on the back. You deserve it!

CHAPTER 14

May

Important Dates

MAY 1 — *May Day*

MAY 2 — *Backwards Day*

MAY 5 — *Cinco de Mayo*

MAY 9 — *Smoky the Bear Day*

MAY 12 — *Kite Day, Limerick Day*

MAY 14 — *National Dance Like A Chicken Day*

Monthly Themes

Mother's Day – *Second Sunday*

Memorial Day – *Fourth Monday*

National Teacher Day – *Tuesday of the first full week (Teacher Appreciation Week)*

National Pet Week
2nd Week in May (Stuffed Pet Parade in class)

Physical Fitness Month

As I type this last month, tears begin to flow when I think of my Superstars. Yes, I know the tears are always flowing, but I can't help it. We have gotten to know each other's strengths and weaknesses. We know how to make each other laugh and cry. I am so proud of them and all of the skills they have mastered in first grade. I have grown to love each one of them differently as if they were my own children. It is now time that they move on to the next grade and you want to give them something so that they will remember their first-grade experience forever.

So in mid-May, I head over to one of my favorite craft stores, Michaels, and I purchase wooden picture frames for $1. These frames hold a 3x5 picture. The sides of the frame are wide enough to write on. I have tons of fabric paint, but I always buy more just in case I run out, which I never do...LOL!! This fabric 3-D paint is used to write on T-shirts, but it works great on wooden frames as well. I also purchase two cans of glossy spray paint, one in hot pink and the other in blue. I spray the frames all pink for the girls and all blue for my boys.

While the paint is drying for a few days on the frames, I think about what each child had done throughout the year...good and not so good. I use their names in an acrostic poem, using their initials to describe what they are to me and what they can aspire to be. There are some students who may not have displayed the best behavior, but this is where I encourage them to be all they can be with adjectives. This affirmation will be written, and they can look at it and may even change their behavior as they look to receive their new picture frame.

Now that the paint is dry on the frames, I write their names down on the left side of the frame in white. I choose a different color paint to write an adjective that goes with the letter. On the other side of the frame, I write the name of the school, the year, and the grade in black along with my name. There is still a lot of space on the frame, so at the top, I draw clouds, a sun, rainbows, birds, or whatever I can think of at the moment. At the very bottom, I draw pictures to represent each girl...balloons, flowers, butterflies, lollipops, just think girlie and cute. For the boys, my freehand drawing is not the greatest, but I draw cars, dinosaurs, basketballs, footballs, or soccer balls. I add numbers, addition, educational words, and whatever else to make it memorable and nice. Be sure when you are drawing that your arm does not smear the paint. I let this dry for several days.

While I am waiting a few days for the frames to dry, I take pictures with each child. Of course, they have no clue why. They know I love to take pictures, so this isn't any different from any other day. I then go to CVS and print each picture from my phone at the kiosk. You will have to cut the picture because they only come in 4x6. I take the cardboard part of the frame and measure the square of our faces. I cut around that part to make the picture fit perfectly in the frame. You can go to my YouTube channel - Forever First Grade to see how I make these. Super easy.

In my class, I have an award ceremony at the end of the year. I find awards for each child whether it is the best smile, great handwriting, math genius, or perfect speller. Certificates that show each child that they are special and have done an excellent job in first grade. The certificates always boost their confidence and lets them know that they are indeed Superstars. I make sure that each child is present that day. After I give out all of the awards, I tell them I have a special treat for them. It is something they should cherish and hold on to for the rest of their lives.

I begin to call each student to present their picture frame of the two of us. I read each frame and tell them what they mean to me and how great of a student they are and how I will certainly miss them. Oh boy, the smiles on their faces and the tears that are welling in my eyes... PRICELESS!! It brings so much joy to

Your students are listening to every word you say. Make those words count.

pass these out. I am proud of them. This is the last celebration party of the year. One year, I decided to pass the frames out at the school end-of-the-year award ceremony...it was a tear-fest for me and the other teachers.

Over the years, I have had parents come up to me and say that their child still says I'm his/her favorite teacher and the picture I gave them is still on their dresser. I smile because I know that I did everything in my power to make first grade memorable. One story from a parent that really was funny was they were going on summer vacation and her son was trying to pack the frame to sit on the dresser in the hotel. That made my day. I smile because I pushed each and every student to their fullest potential. I smile because I know we had a great time learning. Our learning was FUN!! They truly became Superstars!

Another short story that had me in tears is a parent who was substituting at our school happened to be at the Honors program the school was having. She said she watched me get up there in tears and speak about each student with such passion and love. She said that I was so impressive, she could just tell how much I love what I do by taking time out to hand-make 27 picture frames for my students.She went on to say that that's how all teachers should be. She said she could tell that teaching was in my blood. The things I said about each student made her even shed a tear. She shared my excitement and wished that I had taught one of the children. I really cried that day because I had a challenging year with 27 students, and I didn't know how the year was going to turn out. Thanks to my parents, my aide, and staff at school, I made it. I love what I do because I've always dreamed of it. I would not be happy doing anything else.

So, as you plan your year, think of things that will have a lasting effect on your students. Be fun, be happy, and be silly. They love it. After you have established your classroom rules and your students are following them, you can be all of those things. Teach with rigor. Ask those higher-order questions, prod them to answer questions using the vocabulary from the content you taught. Plan those lessons that they will remember. Differentiate for those students who need it. Most of all, be creative. Think out of the box. Think about how you were as a student and the things you needed as a student. You are trusted with young minds that you can form and mold into surgeons, teachers, lawyers, or whatever career they choose. Love what you do, make it awesome, and don't forget to celebrate your students. Every milestone, every test passed, every concept learned, and even homework that is turned in on time. Celebrate! I believe in having fun while learning. They remember it the most and you will become a staple in their minds from now on. Just like I'll never forget my third-grade teacher and all the fun we had. I was so lucky to have her for fourth grade as well. She is etched in my brain forever.

**10 Additional Ideas
To Create A Superstar School Year**

1. Find Ways to Celebrate and Go All Out
2. Communication with Parents
3. The Garden Café
4. Quiet Zones (Reading Under Trees)
5. Importance of Color Schemes
6. Go the Extra Mile
7. Recipes/Nutrition
8. Cross Curricular
9. Music-Fun Friday
10. Fun Ways to Line Up

CHAPTER 15

Find Ways to Celebrate and Go All Out

Your students will remember you when you celebrate milestones and accomplishments in class. There are many holidays and reasons to celebrate throughout the year, along with passing a test or following directions in the hallways or cafeteria. I can think of 10 right off the top of my head, I'm sure there are many more.

I like to WOW my students. When there are special days, I make them extra special. Here are six ways I make memorable days with my students. Some of these celebrations are not academic, but they sure are fun and show school spirit. Celebrating academic success just makes it more memorable and even more exciting. Your parents will get on board. They love for you to make their child feel special and when they come home talking about celebrations, it's the icing on the cake.

1. Spirit Week

Some teachers think Spirit Week is just for the kids, NOT! You are a part of the school spirit. If you don't encourage your students to love their school, then they won't. Lead by example. Dress up. Participate as much as you can. Here I am on several spirit weekdays. I sometimes purchase outfits when the season is over, just so I can have them on hand. I go

to the thrift stores to find items that I can use. Disney Character Day, Super Hero Day, 80's Day, Red Carpet Day, Crazy Hair Day, and Wacky Tacky Day are all the days I've dressed up. When I tell you the students love it, they LOVE IT! Those students who do not participate on the first day come dressed up for the rest of the week. Have fun with your students. They deserve it and so do you!

2. 100th Day of School

On this day, I asked all of the students to come dressed as if they were 100 years old. The surprise was, they didn't know I would come dressed as a one-hundred-year-old, too. I was unrecognizable. I went to the thrift store, found some clothes that I thought a one-hundred-year-old would wear. I even bought a walker. I watched YouTube videos on how to make yourself look older. I followed the video and boy did I look like an old lady. I was in character all day long. By the end of the day, my back really ached.

On this day, I wanted everything to be about the number 100. I made a wonderful banner that hung outside my door saying, Mrs. Holland's Class Is 100 Days Smarter. For our activities for the day, I had four stations for the students to rotate in. They were making a fruit loop necklace out of 100 fruit loops, make a 100th-day headband, complete 100 exercises, and 100th-day photo

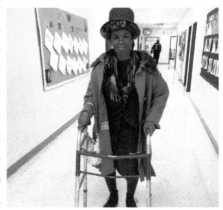

booth. I had a student intern in my class. She made our photo booth for us. It was a poster board cut out with lots of cute stuff on it including the number 100. The day was awesome. One to never forget. All of these activities are very easy to find. Google it. Make Google your friend. These ideas are not all my ideas, but when I find what  I am looking for, I definitely know how to make them my own. You can do the same.

3. Cinco de Mayo

This is a history lesson. We learn about why Cinco de Mayo exists and what it means to the Americans and Mexicans. So why not have a fiesta!! Decorate your room, eat food that is indigenous to that country, and dress up. It's always a celebration going on in the 1st Grade Superstars classroom. My students and I danced and listened to Mexican music. We made maracas out of white paper plates. We decorated the plate. I stapled the sides for them. They then added beans to make noise and then I stapled it shut. I bought a piñata, we wore sombreros and had a blast commemorating the day the Mexicans defeated the French army. I also bought little mustaches for the boys and flowers for the girls to wear in their hair. It was a fiesta to remember.

4. Summer Field Trip

I know you may not want to see your students during the summer, but this is a fun idea. There are so many great movies that come out in the summer. I send a text to my parents to see who is in town. I tell them that I want to go on a summer field trip with their kids, but they have to come too. We meet at the movies. The students are so excited to see the teacher in the summer. You make the students happy and the parents. You can also do this with older students. Go to dinner, lunch, the mall, bowling, or even skating.

5. First Day of School

I celebrate at the beginning of the school year. I know I gave ideas for that. But going into a new grade can be scary, especially for first graders. I read a book called the *First Day Jitters* by Julie Danneberg. In this book, it talks about reasons students may have jitters. So, to end the book, I tell them that I have something that will take all of their jitters away forever. When Superstars drink this juice something magical happens. They are wondering what it is. I tell them that it is called Jitter Juice. I let them know that when they taste it, the bubbles that are in the juice will take away all of the butterflies, worries, and doubts of being in first grade. Everyone gets a cup and we toast the jitters away. The recipe is simple: apple juice, and fizzy clear soda... Sprite, or gingerale. You can even add some sherbet to it to make it extra special. They ask for that juice all year long. You can even offer it for the first time they take a test.

6. Birthdays

Birthdays are reasons to celebrate. Be sure to display a birthday chart in your room. On my calendar, each month I put the child's name on the day of their birthday. They love when I change it each month when they can see their names. On their birthday, I give a crown for each student to wear for the day. I put their names big on it for all to see. They are extremely excited about wearing the crown. I buy the crowns from Really Good Stuff, another favorite online store. On this day, they also get to tell about their favorite things and bring in a Show-n-Tell.

Communication With Parents

It is so important that there is open communication with parents.

Parents want to know that you are approachable and that you will answer their calls or emails. Parents are entrusting their precious commodity with you and they just want to feel that their kids are safe with you. In all of my years of teaching, I have never had a bad run-in with a parent. Ok, one.

On parent night, I give everyone my personal cell phone number and email address. I know that some teachers will never do this, but I want parents to have it because I want them to feel free to contact me at any time they need to. Well, not anytime, but you understand where I am coming from. I let them know that I go to bed early, so after 8, please don't call or text. My wish is respected. I am sure to get their numbers as well. The lines of communication are open.

On this night, I also give my parents a syllabus. This syllabus has the rules for the class, names of the books and curriculum we will use for the year, pictures of my class and students, and the class schedule. I send a daily email. I talk about the day, important info for the week, homework, or whatever I deem necessary. I am very friendly and down-to-earth in my emails. Parents tell me that they look forward to getting my emails. Sometimes they find them quite funny and inspirational. Wellll, my nighttime job is a comedian...hehehehehe! I teach first grade, so I know sometimes pertinent information may not reach home. So by the time they get home, the parents already know what to expect because they received my email.

Each Friday, I send home a Study Guide, or some may call it "Week at a Glance." In this guide are the things we will cover for the following week. I include the memory verse, spelling words, and sentence dictation. If there is a test that Friday, I include items to study. I get my template for the study guide from one of my favorite teacher sites, Super Teacher Worksheets. There are an abundant amount of resources on this site for teachers, even down to creating your test. The best thing about it is, it saves everything you make. This way, you don't have to recreate it. You can even go back to edit it for the next year. It really teaches you to work smarter and easier.

Keep your parents abreast of everything. Please don't give them a reason to complain. As a parent myself, I am always happy when I know ahead of time what to expect for my child. If it is homework, a project due, a test, or even what to wear to school, I want to know these things ahead of time. I know that there may be a calendar that I can go to, but getting that email to remind me of what to do is even better. Eventually, we want to make our children and students responsible to bring homework home and other pertinent information, but in the beginning, I find it necessary to be kept in the know by the teacher.

Dupont Garden Café

The reason I came up with the Dupont Garden Cafe is that the students were absolutely out of control in the multi-purpose room during lunchtime. This was not only my class, but up to three other classes shared this space. No matter how many times the teachers would say, "quiet down, be quiet, don't get up without permission, it was still mayhem in there.

This room is used for everything, assembly, worship, morning care, dismissal, and lunch. I never wanted to go in there because the noise level was insanely loud. I would have a headache every time I left there. The students were eating with their mouths open, throwing food, and just out of control. Mind you, this is supposed to be "my lunch break" but I had to eat with students. I at least wanted to come in and eat my food in some type of order and quietness.

So, I couldn't take it anymore. One day, I decided I would turn the multi-purpose room into a Garden Café. I know that a lot of students have been to restaurants, so they know what the atmosphere is like there. Customers are not jumping out of their seats, throwing food, chewing with their mouths open, or talking loudly. So, I went to my principal and told her my idea and she said go for it.

At the time, all I knew is that I wanted the multi-purpose room to mimic a restaurant. What could I do to get the students on board and to follow rules in this big room? In a restaurant, tables are set and there may be a flower on the table or candles. So, I asked for money to purchase tablecloths, flowers, and vases to put them in. I also bought baskets to put forks, spoons, knives, and napkins in. I made sure that the sound system was always hooked up to play smart music (Mozart, elevator music). Of course, this music would calm them as soon as they walked in (high hopes)...LOL!

I had the administrative secretary create this huge sign that said Dupont Park Garden Café. It had flowers and vines on it, very beautiful. It would cover the back wall of the room. In the days coming up to the grand opening of the Garden Café, teachers were told to discuss with the students the importance of lunchroom etiquette. We all were on the same page, so all students had the same information. The rules for this café would be on the door upon entering and on the walls in several places throughout the room. No excuses for misbehavior.

> Of course with all the work you do with your students, find a way to display it so everyone can see.

On the morning of the grand opening, all students were gathered together again to implement the rules and expected behavior in the Garden Café. They sounded very excited about this café. They were asking questions and wanted to know if they could buy food in the café. Now, that sparked another idea for the students. So, I told them, if the first few weeks went well, then maybe the café would start selling items.

All of the kids went back to their classes and that's when parent volunteers, a few teachers who had a break, and I went to work. We rearranged the tables restaurant style. We put the tablecloths and centerpieces of flowers in vases on the tables. The baskets were filled with utensils on the tables. Having the utensils on the table would eliminate unnecessary walking around. Everything was within the student's reach. Garbage cans were placed near each table. There were name cards for each class and salt and pepper shakers. The teachers even had a table of their own. The Garden Café was coming to life. Once we put the music on, it was serene. I began to dance around and cry (if you know me), so happy that the students would get to experience this café. It was beautiful.

And now for the revealing of The Dupont Park Garden Café....you should have seen the big eyes, smiley faces, the oooh's and ahhhh's. They absolutely loved it!! They followed the rules for warming up food and practiced their table etiquette. I heard pass the napkins, please. I heard thank you. All of the manners they practiced were being used. The music played in the background and each student spoke with their inside voices to the person next to them. They practiced and obeyed all of the rules for two weeks, so I had to keep my promise and start selling food in the café. We sold chips, pickles, drinks, and on special days, I would sell fruit smoothies, make pancakes, or nachos and cheese.

The moral of the story, if you want to see a change in students, you must do something about it. Set an example and they'll follow. Show them how to be on their best behavior. Saying be quiet, sit down, don't do this, or that does not work. I put them in an environment that shaped their behavior to change for the better. They loved the café and did everything in their power to keep it.

Eventually, students were the ones who ran the café. They were able to leave class 10 minutes early to set the tables, get the café items ready to sell, and make sure everything was in place. Of course classwork had to be completed. Class name cards were removed, and students were able to sit where they wanted. They earned it! This café worked and I am so proud that the students were given the opportunity to show that they can have great behavior and follow through with lessons they learned about lunchroom etiquette.

Quiet Zones: Reading Under Trees

I love to read. My guilty pleasure reading is trashy novels, oh boy do I hate saying that. I love to read when it is quiet and in a place that makes reading relaxing. I love to imagine the stories and put myself in them...ok not the trashy ones...LOL!!! I can read a book in a day if I have the time. Once I start, I can't stop reading until the book is finished. Getting to learn about new characters and new places always makes me happy. I always want to instill in my students a love for reading. I make it as exciting as I can. I have them close their eyes as I am reading and imagine that they were in the story. We discuss how our voices should sound when reading. Making your voice go high at the end of a sentence that has a question mark. Pausing at commas and stopping at periods.

I get them excited about the exploration of each book or story that we read. Mrs. Dickerson, parent, who happened to be a teacher at the school I teach in always tells me how her son loves to read out loud and uses all of the inflections he learned in class. She knows he got it from me because he can mimic me to a tee. He says, "Your voice is supposed to sound like this after you read a sentence with a question mark"...LOL That makes me happy to know that he was listening and can be outside of class using what he has learned.

One year, when I was deciding how I wanted to set up my reading center, I was at the park. I was actually sitting under a tree reading and my mind wandered to my classroom, as it does so often. I decided that day that I wanted a tree in my classroom. I didn't know how I would get a tree in my class. There was a parent at my school who was always volunteering to do things around the school. He did everything from helping to fry French fries, building stages, and the plumbing. Everyone should have a Mr. Cabico at their school...and he's a firefighter. So, I texted Mr. Cabico and told him my idea. He said he'd be up to the school later on and if I could sketch out what I wanted; he was sure he could help me out.

I was eagerly waiting for him to arrive at school, so I could show him my tree idea. I'm not an artist, but I knew what I wanted. He saw my sketch and said that's easy. He told me he had some plywood laying around that would work perfectly for the tree. I said plywood, ok I didn't exactly know what it was, don't laugh, so he told me it would work. I trusted him. I was going to get me a tree...yayyy!!

The next day, Mr. Cabico comes into my classroom with this 8ft tall tree. It was perfect!!! OMG! I was so excited. I asked him how much I owed him, and he said nothing. My son will be in your class this year, so it's my gift to you. Look at God! He knows teachers live on a budget...LOL! I was so appreciative of it. If you know me, I cried. I immediately had him take it to the art teacher and she painted it for me. It was even more beautiful. I finally had my tree.

After it dried, I called Mr. Cabico and asked him to mount it on the wall for me. Of course, he did it without any hesitation. I had the perfect corner for it. Now, my hunt to find the perfect grass to put under my awesome tree. I searched the web looking for the exact one and came across a green carpet at IKEA. I got over there so quick. It was a plush kelly-green color and perfect. I bought it with my $150 teacher budget that we get and rushed to put it under the tree. If you know me, yep I cried at just the thought of my students sitting under the tree reading. This tree became the welcome tree, an apple

The Reading Tree.

tree, it was a Christmas tree, with each theme for the month, the tree changed. It was the best place for my students to come and read a book sitting on a pillow on the green grass. I loved it and so did my students. Making reading fun and enjoyable for my students is very important to me. Making them comfortable while they are reading is the icing on the cake. I have changed schools and classrooms, but my tree goes wherever I go.

Importance of Color Schemes

I love primary colors. Primary colors are so bright, and they bring any dull room to life. I taught at a small school with not many resources. I was given a room that was a nice size, but it had no color anywhere from the previous teacher. She had an old file cabinet that was grey, the cabinets were beige, and it was just not an inviting place for students to come and learn, to me. So, I used the money that was given to each teacher and I bought the paint. I couldn't afford to buy new furniture, soooo the next best thing was colorful paint. I painted each drawer on the cabinet a different color. I painted the cabinets along the wall a different primary color. The room was beginning to come alive. I could now see myself in there teaching with a few more extras added.

I then began to fill the walls with colorful posters because I could not paint the walls. It may have been too bright for some, but for students, it was the best place to be. Studies indicate that color plays a role in emotion, productivity, and communication, and

learning (School Planning and Management, July 2009). Creating an environment conducive to learning is key. Colors do in fact have meanings, such as large amounts of reds and oranges can cause overstimulation. On the other, hand blues and greens cause students to feel calm, relaxed, and happy. I have a yellow couch in my room, which can elicit a feeling of liveliness, energy, and happiness. I am a lively person and my room reflects my personality: colorful. So when you come to my class, put your sunshades on. It's all about the students and how they will be able to thrive and feel a sense of safety, security, and happiness in my room where they are eager to learn. My classroom is a place that students love to come to but hate to leave.

Go The Extra Mile

Teachers expect their students to turn in the perfect papers and projects. But are teachers teaching to perfection? Are you teaching lessons that are creative and innovative? Do you prepare a lesson with your students in mind or do you just copy it from the book, going page by page? When I am preparing my lesson plans, I go the extra mile. Of course, I use the book, but it limits my creativity. When you know your students' needs, you should be able to look at what's in the book and differentiate it for your students. I know that I want them to not only learn a concept, but I want them to remember it for a lifetime. So, I may come dressed as the Statue of Liberty to get my point across. Not only am I triggering two of their senses, but they will also be able to learn all about the USA monuments because I was visible, and I got their attention.

My son was given an assignment during Black History Month. He only had to write a paper on George Washington Carver. Simple, right, not! I'm a drama momma and over the top. I wanted my son to not only get a great grade but to always remember who this very important Black Historian was. By the way, he was only in second grade. We began to research this man and he began to ask questions about him. I had him find the answers and he began to write his paper. He was very interested in all of the inventions he created and even said he might want to become a scientist when he grew up.

The paper was finished, and it was time to present it. We decided that when it was his turn, he would present as George Washington Carver. We bought him a lab coat, found a microscope, made him a mustache, and put white talcum powder in his hair to make it white, just like Carver. He presented his paper with no paper. He was able to tell all about Carver as Carver. His teacher thought this was excellent. And of course, he got 100%. It's not as important to me that he got 100%, but that he knows exactly who he wrote about. To this day, he can tell you everything about Carver, including dates. That's my boy. The students in the class also got a visual of who Carver was and could remember details about him as well. I teach him to go far and beyond the assignment. That's how teachers should be. Go far and beyond to get your point across to your students. Bring your lessons to life at all costs. Be animated, be excited about the lesson. When you are teaching you are on stage. All eyes are on you. You can't be boring. You have to capture their attention in the first 5 minutes. Spark their prior knowledge and get their knowledge juices flowing. And I'll bet they'll remember those lessons for a lifetime. That's what being a Superstar is all about!

Recipes/Nutritional Learning

I find that teaching students to cook helps promote healthy food choices. At my previous school, I was head of the nutrition guild. In college, I had only one class to complete to receive a minor in Nutrition, therefore allowing me to teach simple food preparation classes to students. We had such a wonderful curriculum that I developed to teach once a week. Students were lined up for this guild because they knew in this guild, we would not only be cooking and eating, but also learning how to make healthy food choices. I'm sure it was more of the first part, but nevertheless, the lines were long.

In this guild, I incorporated cross-curricular assignments in math, science, and language arts. The students learned to measure (math), food pyramid (science), and how to write recipes (LA), which included so many different elements. The only challenging thing about teaching these students, was that the school did not have a kitchen. That's right, no kitchen. So, I had to be creative and improvise each week to make these lessons spectacular. But believe you me, we cooked every week. Now that I am not teaching guild, I

still include nutrition and cooking in my lessons. Once a month, I find a reason to cook in my class.

Just like Physical Education is important for kids' well-being, so is nutrition. I teach my students to make healthy choices when deciding whether to eat chips or a halo. I set the example by bringing fruit to snack on. Now instead of bringing me candy, they are happy to give me fruit instead. Sometimes, I think they are trying to get rid of the fruit their parents give them and give it to me...LOL. But I accept it and eat it. Especially when they found out that I love grapes and those little tangerines called Halos, my desk would be filled with them every day.

My classroom is a place that students love to come to but hate to leave.

Kids love pizza and it's a quick go-to for parents. One lesson I taught my students is how to make great pizza, but at home. Instead of using white, dough, use wheat. Instead of pepperoni, use turkey pepperoni. At my local grocery store, they make pizza, so I knew I would be able to purchase dough already made. I bought several balls, wheat, and white. My school has a no meat policy, so I couldn't do meat, so I went crazy with vegetables. We discussed each of their nutritional values and how they can help us be healthy. We used both types of dough to see if the taste would be different if we used wheat.

Some kids were picky about which veggies they wanted to eat, but I told them, if they were not allergic to any of the veggies, everyone had to taste everything, or they could not participate in making the pizza. What a way to get 100% participation. This school had a kitchen, we got permission to use it. We wore our aprons, rolled out the dough, and went to town making our pizzas. The end products were tasty, and they looked appetizing. After eating the pizzas, we compared the white flour to the wheat flour. Remember, everyone had to taste both crusts. We got out our Venn Diagrams and found how they were alike, different, and the same. The students were pleasantly surprised that the wheat crust didn't taste any different from the white crust. They basically taste the same, but the color was different. So, you see how turning a simple day of making a pizza can be a lesson all in itself.

I have cooked many meals in my classes, with the students' help. It gives them a sense of awareness about nutrition and how to get around in a kitchen at an early age. We have baked cupcakes, made soup, made a pot of beans, baked bread, and even made popcorn balls. We have also made clay dough in class if you want to call that cooking... LOL!

I know that cooking can't happen all the time in your classes but try to include it as much as possible. It makes a well-rounded kid

and you should see their confidence level rise when they are stirring a pot or helping to roll dough. The goal is to make lifelong learners and learning to cook, measure, or make healthy choices in food is only the beginning of their memories.

Cross-Curricular Math and Social Studies

Counting money is not a required standard for first grade, but I introduce money to them anyway. I noticed that counting money is on the standardized tests, so it's a good thing to know the value of the coins. I try to make it easy for them to understand. I have the big coins that I laminate and put magnets behind them. I also have plastic coins for them to play with in centers.

The best way I found to teach students about money is to use real coins. We discuss the shape, size, and color of each. I explain to them that because they know how to count by ones, fives, and tens, it makes it easier for them to count. They just have to recognize the different coins.

After we have had several weeks of learning to count money, I tell them that I will open up a store in the classroom for them to buy things. This store will be called 1st Grade Superstars Super Store. I have a treasure chest with supplies, toys, cars, and all sorts of trinkets I have found and collected. The only way they can purchase something from the store is that they have to know how to count their money to pay for the items they want. So, of course, they are going home to practice counting with their parents. The day the Superstar Store opens, they are ready and excited to purchase items with their own money. Those who have not mastered this skill receive a little help, one on one with me. No one is turned away. They love it. It encourages them to keep track of their money and learn to count it.

While learning to count money, in Social Studies we are learning about our community. We are learning about services and goods that are offered in communities. While searching for an idea to make a cross-curricular activity come to life, the 2nd-grade class right next door opened a Market. They had Market Day where each student chose either a good to sell or provide a service to sell that the community needed. They had to advertise their good or service by making signs to hang from their desks. They each brought in their good to sell or the items for their service. It was a day to remember. The students sold cookies, dolls, cupcakes, candy, bracelets, and books. The services were face painting, massages, tattoos, counseling, and more. I'm sure, learning to count money helped them set a price and actually use their money to buy on Market Day. Kudos to Mrs. Hong.

This activity can turn into a fundraiser for your school. Each class can sell a service or a good during the school year. Market Day can exist for the entire school. This also can be an economics lesson as well.

Music Fun Friday

I was told by a parent who overheard another parent say that all my students do is play in my class. I was hurt by that comment. So, I decided I would call this parent and give her piece of my mind. But instead of letting her have it, I asked her the reason why she thought such a thing. She went on to tell me that her daughter always says she has so much fun every day. She'll ask what she learned in school today and she would tell her that they were jumping around dancing and singing during math, spelling, or science.

As I listened to her go on about dancing and singing, I asked her if she asked her child why they were up dancing and singing around the class and she said no. I then told her, yes, we play and have fun in my class every day. I told her she had a right to be concerned if her child was playing every day. I asked her to ask her child some addition and subtraction facts, I asked her to ask her child to spell some of her spelling words. I asked her did she have to help her child with her homework each night?

Every lesson that I teach, I want to make it fun and enjoyable. There's a reason for my playing. I'm not a stiff teacher, so usually, you will find me singing and marching around the room with my students. We're not just marching around playing, but we are moving our bodies learning facts, our spelling words, what a noun or verb is. I find that for me if I move my body a certain way while learning something, I can recall it quicker. So, with my students, there are students who are kinesthetic learners and they learn by doing, so moving and playing with certain manipulatives helps them to master concepts. They in turn remember them. During the test, I hear my students chanting and singing songs we made up during the week to help with recollection.

After my explanation of why we play, I thought she was satisfied with my answers, but she wasn't. So, she says, well what's Fun Friday? I'm paying tuition for 5 days a week, not four days. I say, of course, I want you to get your money's worth at this school. So, I then had to explain to her why we have Fun Friday. Usually, Friday's is the day most teachers test their students. This day can be so stressful for students that it makes them not excel on the test they are taking. Well, in my class with the First Grade Superstars, we look forward to Fun Friday...which is Test Day! This is the day my students prove to me that they are ready to give back to me what I have taught them all week. They know that we will celebrate what they have learned, and we do this by recalling information which is testing. By calling this day Fun Friday, it takes the pressure off students to allow them to think that test-taking isn't such a bad thing. You have learned the information, so show me what you know.

Before we get started with our test, I explain, I put on music. This music is music to make them want to move their bodies and dance. They always say, "play your songs, play Virtue" (shameless plug...LOL). I am the Superstar teacher, so why not!! They are out of their seats marching around, singing, dancing, having fun because we are about to take our test. They don't know that moving around is an effective cognitive strategy to help strengthen learning, improve memory and retrieval, and enhance learner motivation and morale. They are just dancing because in their minds it's fun. This goes on for about 15 minutes. Then we sit and take our tests, and voila...everyone aces the tests. It's a strategy all teachers should adopt. I even sneak and do it during standardized tests... shhhh... don't tell...LOL!

I use music for everything. I make up songs so that students can remember what a noun is, what a verb is: a verb is something that you do, oh yeah, something that you do, oh yeah! They have songs and body movements for what a short vowel is, what a long vowel is. They go home singing these made-up songs, but they stick in their little-wittle brains and they can recall this information. That's most important, right?

So, my parent is finally satisfied with the reason we "play" in first grade. I bet one thing; her child was certainly ready for second grade. She was on a 3.8 grade in reading and a 2.9 grade average in math by the end of first grade. Bamm! I have the data to prove that playing can be successful.

Fun Ways To Line Up

I turn everything into a lesson. How you line your class up is vital, well in my case it was. There is always that one or two students who have to be first in line EVERYTIME we line up. This student would always push and shove, knock you down, or hit you to be in that first position, geeez! Do you have students like this? Well when school starts, I am sure to create a boy and girl line. I put pink feet on the floor for the girls and there are blue feet on the floor for the boys. The words Line Up are above each pair of feet. I use clear contact paper to be sure the feet stay in place all year long on the floor. The boys are on one side and the girls on the other side.

There are mini-lessons throughout the whole year. When we learn about ordinal numbers, alphabetical order, and height (shortest to tallest or tallest to shortest), that's when I switch up the lines. I had the most problems with boys lining up, my girls seemed to always have it together. I always tell the boys, ladies are first, no matter what. Being a gentleman will get you places in life. So, they are willing to let the girls go first without a fuss.

The lesson comes in when the students have to get themselves in the proper order. They can figure out

> I'm not a stiff teacher, so usually you will find me singing and marching around the room with my students.

who's the shortest and go from there. They have to figure out who would be first if we went by first names or last names. Somedays, I line them up by their group (table they sit at). One day, I had them line up from youngest to oldest. This was of course after we did the timeline of our birthdays in the class. They remembered that there was a timeline across the front of the class and went from there. The trick was, there was a boy and a girl line. But they did well. I really tripped them up, when one day they came to class and there was a pink foot and a blue foot that said line-up. They were looking for their individual lines. I then used those same mini lessons for the entire class. They lined up by height, ABC order, and they even lined up in XYZ order. The confusion came when they said, I thought you said girls were always first...LOL, but these are just a few ways you can have fun lining your class up.

CHAPTER 16

Superstar Thank You's

It has been over 12 years since I have been back in the classroom full-time. I limited my singing with Virtue to traveling only on the weekend. So, I am still from the classroom to the stage. The love that I have for teaching goes beyond what I imagined as a child. I knew that I wanted to be a teacher, but the extent of it has exceeded my imagination.

The first class I taught had 24 students and included in that 24 were a set of triplets. I was excited and scared all at the same time. With 24 students come 24 different personalities and levels. I had a TA, but I was always so protective and possessive of my students I barely let her do anything. I went through three TA's that year and ended up with one who I could trust. I wanted to make sure that each student, although there were so many of them, got what they needed. I felt that if I didn't give my all, their parents' money would go to waste. I never wanted any parent to blame me for a child not learning. This class was a loving class. They were kind to each other and wanted to please me. We sang, danced, marched, played, and most of all learned all of the first-grade standards and more. My principal Miss Q said, "I ROCKED 1st Grade". She always reminded me, that's the reason I hired you. I knew you would go above and beyond. My observation results were proficient and distinguished. I always had a smile from ear to ear.

Every year is not going to be a walk in the park. You will have students who will challenge you. They will challenge you, behaviorally and academically. Each year, I have had those students who challenge your patience. Those students who have been labeled "bad" are my favorites. I make sure they are kept busy. I let them be the classroom helper. I encourage and praise great behavior when I see that the student has tried. I'm not the type of teacher who calls parents every day for a child in my class who misbehaves. I tell this to my parents at the beginning of the school year. I would hate to get a call during the day that the teacher was not able to solve a problem with behavior in class. Of course, there are ones that need special attention from the principal. I let parents know that if they get a call or email from me, it was something I was totally not able to handle.

There was a kid who was coming to my class the following year who had a history of behavior problems. I made up my mind that I did not want the teachers to tell me anything negative about this child. I wanted them to only tell me how he was academically. I wanted to get to know him for myself with a clean slate. I realized within the first week of school that he would challenge me with disruptive behaviors. I immediately began to pray that I wouldn't have a whole year of this. I told him that I thought he was a smart kid and I knew that he could show me he could be a Superstar.

I went home and assigned each student jobs for the class. I noticed that he enjoyed his job and was good at it. He was a very bright student, so he was always first to finish his work and it was done correctly and neat. I took note of that and challenged him a bit more with his classwork.

After three weeks of school, his mother called me to ask was everything ok with her son. I said, of course, why? She said that she was so used to getting phone calls or emails that she thought something was wrong. I began to explain to her that her son was doing extremely well, and if there was something that I could not handle in the class, I would let her know. She went on to say, did the other teachers tell you about him. I said, no. I told her that I wanted to get to know her son for myself and whatever he did before me didn't matter. He had a clean slate with me. She was so surprised that I said that and said, well call me if you need me.

The year passed and she received two phone calls from me. They both were because he injured himself on the playground. Her son became the Superstar he knew he could be. He was polite, he used his manners, and his behavior was A-1. I gave this student the benefit of the doubt and didn't let what I heard about him cause me to treat him differently. He had a blank slate and filled it with all good things.

On every holiday, my birthday, random days, his mother gave me gifts. At the end of the year, I had to have someone help me carry all of the gifts she gave me to my car. She even asked me to move to the next grade with him. She said she could finally be at work and be at peace knowing her child was behaving.

I want my students to trust me. I want to build a relationship with them where they know I have their best interest at heart. All problems will be solved in the classroom. Don't worry about me telling your parents. They know the rules and I expect them to follow them. Those students who push the envelope will get privileges taken away. This usually solves those problems. They know that the 1st grade Superstars always have fun learning and they did not want to miss out on any of it.

Then there are students who suffer academically. Your head hurts trying to figure out what you can do to get through. Sometimes, there is nothing you can do, and you need to have that conversation with the principal and parents. Don't be afraid to ask for help. Get the professional reading specialist or math specialist to help you navigate through this. It's OK. When you have done all you can do, there's help. Never feel that you are a failure. I've been there, and thinking that makes it worst. You are a better teacher for recognizing it.

I pray that something you have read can and will help you to be a master Superstar teacher. All of these ideas were not created by me, there is nothing new under the sun. But what I have done is make these ideas my own and created resources and activities that would benefit my class. When I was in college, I remember one of my favorite teachers, Professor Warren telling me that I was very creative, and I thought out of the box. She told me that my love for children and learning came naturally. I had an assignment to create an educational game board for students. I thought, oh my! How will I do that? I remembered the game Candy Land and went on from there on how I'd create my game board. I found poster board, foam board, and cardboard until I found the right base. Then I ended up using the lid to a big shoe box, it was perfect. I drew in all the lanes with different colors and put pictures of ABC's and 123's on it. I came up with the rules, the playing cards, and pieces to move around the board. This game turned out fabulous. I was so proud to present it to the class. You see, I didn't copy Candy Land, I used it as a guide to help me create my own game board. You can do the same. Don't reinvent the wheel, make it work for you. That's what I did. Boy, I wish I knew where that game was right now. I'd certainly use it in my class now.

When all you can think of is how you can become a better teacher, or what ways you can better assist a student is all that consume your mind, then this is the job for you. You must be passionate, caring, and innovative, but most of all creative. You may have been a teacher for more than 20 years, but there still are new things that you can learn to help you teach smarter and leave your work at school. Don't be so set in your ways that your way is the best way. Get out there and find some continuing education classes to help ignite that spark again. I know you may be tired, but your students depend on you to have energy and to go the extra mile to make learning fun. You may be a first-year teacher and you're nervous about the school year. Don't be. There are so many resources out there to use. Google will be your best friend. YOU GOT THIS!!

I hope you take these ideas and resources and use them. Celebrate your students and parents. Once a month, find a reason to celebrate other than a birthday party. Celebrate minute math, spelling, reading, or science. Celebrate the end of a chapter. Celebrate that one child who got over a rough patch. Make them feel special, make them feel loved. When students know that you care for them, they want to please you, they want to get good grades. By the end of the year, they will not want to leave your class and when you see them in the hallways, at church, in the park, on the street, or throughout life they'll say, I wish I were back in your class. They will let you know how much of an influence you have been in their lives. The parents will tell you that after all these years, their child still talks about you. They'll say, my child still has the picture of the two of you on his dresser. Those are the words that are important to me. It brings joy to my soul and I can sleep at night knowing that I made a difference in a child's life.

My mother has been so influential in my life. I watched her daily with a 7th grade education, teach me the ways of life single-handedly. Not just me, but my five other siblings as well. We each had a special thing with my mom. She knew how to make each of us feel as though we were the only child, and special. Although she couldn't help me with my homework, she was there to give me support and tell me I can do it. She stayed up late at night with me to complete homework assignments, just for moral support. She made sure that her words were encouraging and helpful. She never wanted me to give up, although there were times when I wanted to. She wanted me to keep going and to make something out of myself. She was energetic and helpful in the best way she knew how to be. She is my hero. She was really my first teacher, and therefore, I have been taught by thee best. Mommy, you kept me covered in prayers. You encouraged me to become the teacher you saw in me before I saw it in myself. You are indeed thee smartest person I know, and I thank you for your example of being a great mom and teacher of all things. I love you so much, Rebecca.

My siblings let me be their teacher, too. I had great students to practice on. To this day, I still try and teach (boss) them and they always say, "you are not my teacher." I am older than the last two, so they had no choice but to let me be their teacher. Thank you, Karima and Heather, for allowing me to boss you around and be your teacher even when you didn't want me to be. Thank you Dionne for teaching me to read even though I bugged you to death...LOL. Thank you for your patience with me when I wanted to read all of your books and you let me. To my brother Peter, even though you are much older, and you were gone to the Air Force when I was little, thank you for always being so kind and proud of all that I did. Thank you for that big baby doll you hid in the closet and I found it before Christmas. She was a great student.

To one of the best students ever, my son Stinger. When I taught you in first grade, I was so nervous. I didn't know how to be your teacher and mommy. I didn't know what you were going to call me. It's so funny, that you never called me mommy and you didn't call me Mrs. Holland. You would just raise your hand or wave it uncontrollably and wait to be called on. I didn't want to show favoritism or treat you bad. I was assigned a mentor named Helen Marshall (a retired teacher) and she helped me to split the difference. That time I made you cry in class, I cried, too. I didn't want the other kids or parents to think I was treating you better than I treated their kids. Mrs. Marshall told me that first, you were my son and I must look out for your feelings and make you most comfortable because it was probably hard for you, too. The day you came home and told me that I was a really good teacher and you really liked me encouraged me so much. I'll never forget your sweet words to me. You helped me to be creative and come up with out of the box ideas because I wanted to please you. I wanted you to be smart, happy, and learn in fun ways. You told me that I was your favorite teacher

> You told me that I was your favorite teacher and you don't know what that did for me.

and you don't know what that did for me. You were in 7th grade and you still remembered the songs I taught you and fun things we did in class. I must have left a great impression on you. For you to see me with two sets of eyes, mommy and teacher and still like me is awesome...LOL! I love you with all of my heart and I pray that you continue to learn and grow up to be the Marine Biologist you said you wanted to be in first grade. OK, I know it changed 50 times, but whatever you decide to be, I'm 100% supportive. Do it with all your might, Superstar style. Never give up trying to reach for the stars.

To my husband, Skip. You are the reason I wrote this book. You encouraged me to put all my knowledge and smarts on paper. You thought everything I did in my classes was creative and innovative and people needed to hear about it. You always pump me up and tell me I am the best teacher you know. Thank you for believing in me and supporting all that I do. You're the best!

I want to end this book saying thank you to my principals Miss Q. (RIP), Dr. Donovan, and Mr. Alberty for allowing me to use my creativity in the classroom. I can't remember a time that I came up with something off the wall and you said no, don't do that. You let me be great and I appreciate you for it.

I want to thank all of my parents for being so supportive of me in the classroom. You never turned me down for donating items, going on field trips to help chaperone, and you never complained. If there was a problem, you brought it to me first and not my principal. Thanks for reading my daily emails. I know I sent a lot of them, LOL! Thank you for trusting me with your children.

And last, but not least thank you to ALL of my students whom I love soooo much. From my early years at Oakwood Elementary/Academy, Madison Mission Academy, and even at the Child Development Lab, where I did my practicum, thank you! To my students at Dupont Park and George E. Peters...yes, I am crying as I type this (sob, sob). You came to school every day. You never wanted to miss a day of school. I have never seen students who were so excited about what they were going to learn the next day, or who never wanted to miss a day of school, even when you were sick. Thank you for letting me fill your blank slates with all that I know. Thank you for challenging me to think of new ways to discipline you. Thank you for staying after school for enrichment. Thank you for being kind and lovable. Thank you for all of the laughter you brought to me. You kids are some funny people. I could write a whole other book on just the things you say to me to make me bust out laughing. Thank you for the hugs, for the kind notes, the pictures, and sweet gifts. Thank you for your willingness to allow me to be creative and use you as my guinea pigs...hehehehe. You had open minds and were willing to go the extra mile. Thank you for coming back after all these years to say thank you or to help me finish my classroom. I could go on and on, but I'll stop. My first two classes are in college now and I hope a few of you choose to be teachers. Always keep an open mind and don't let anyone tell you that you are not smart, because you are. You give me energy; you give me life. Work hard and never stop reaching for the stars. You are a SUPERSTAR... oh yeaaaah! (inserts singing and dancing). I love you all.

Your favorite teacher,
Mrs. Holland... Muahhhh!

Useful Websites

www.superteachers.com

www.writinga-z.com

www.education.com

www.brainpopjr.com

www.brainpop.com

www.lessonplanet.com

www.discoveryeducation.com

www.spellingcity.com

ixl.com

www.teacherspayteachers.com

www.acceleratedreading.com

www.studenttreasures.com (publish a free book)

www.Pinterest.com

GOOGLE: WhatEVER you are looking for, it's there. Google it!

Favorite Stores On Teachers Pay Teachers

Meet Miss Parker

Tiny Teaching Shack

The Moffat Girls

Just A Primary Girl

A Teachable Teacher

Miss Kindergarten Love

Catherine Reed The Brown Bag Teacher

Babbling Abby (great fonts)

Miss Plemons Kindergarten (CCSS Exit Tickets for Math and LA)

Jessica Tobin

Anne Gardner (Great guided reading passages for all levels)

Education with an Apron

The Tutu Teacher

Read Like a Rockstar

Cara Carroll

Tales of Patty Pepper

The Happy Teachers Palette

The Designer Teacher

Life on Stage with Virtue